Reputational Crises Unspun

Tom Schermer

Reputational Crises Unspun

A Stakeholder Solution to Reputational Crises

Springer

Tom Schermer
Brisbane, QLD, Australia

The examples used herein may be partially hypothetical to illustrate various possible strategies.

ISBN 978-981-16-5129-8 ISBN 978-981-16-5130-4 (eBook)
https://doi.org/10.1007/978-981-16-5130-4

This Springer imprint is published by the registered company Springer Nature Singapore Pte Ltd.
The registered company address is: 152 Beach Road, #21-01/04 Gateway East, Singapore 189721, Singapore

Preface

Stakeholders are a problem in a reputational crisis. Because without stakeholders there is no reputational crisis. But if we look at stakeholders differently and then work with them, we can solve the crisis and improve our output and operating environment. If we resituate the stakeholder paradigm, we can explore different ways to viewing crises, and thereby new ways to solving reputational crises and issues.

Organisations and people experience reputational crises every day. The up-to-the-minute social media and online news media feeds let us know the moment someone does something wrong. Often the wrongdoing is of minor significance, but when a reputation reaches crisis point, it can have extreme impacts right across an organisation, its stakeholders, and the organisation's environment.

A reputational crisis can only exist if there are stakeholders. For without stakeholders, there is not a single person to offend, nor lawmakers or legitimate claimants to reparations, nor anyone to influence the crisis. This book explores the tangible and intangible aspects of reputational crises using many practical examples and case studies of what has gone wrong. There is a strong focus on new interpretations of stakeholder theory which allows us to make a better organisation and world in the face of tumultuous and disruptive events.

Following years of research on reputational crises, theoretical and practical, it became apparent that crisis communication research and texts have been too limited to traditional viewpoints. To date, crisis communication has largely overlooked the environments in which these crises occur. Numerous fields of study which are significant to understanding crises have not been engaged with sufficiently and are largely overlooked. These include, but are not limited to, psychology, social psychology, revisiting stakeholder theory, interest groups, and corporate social responsibility. Though specific relevance of these is explained throughout the chapters, the basic ethos of each of these fields are as follows:

Psychology is important to understanding how individual crisis stakeholders feel and how they may be affected. And consequently, what their responses are likely to be.

Social psychology gives us a better understanding of how people work in group dynamics in the context of stakeholder activity in terms of motivation.

Revisiting stakeholder theory is crucial. The founder of contemporary stakeholder theory himself has remodelled stakeholder theory and tried to debunk the most common misunderstandings. It would be short-sighted to design crisis communication strategies and theories based on what now appears to be a wanting stakeholder theory.

Interest groups can now form overnight due to social media and within a week collect enough signatures to persuade a government to change laws. Most crisis communication literature skirt around the concepts of social media. This book explores interest groups and social media stakeholders using the revised stakeholder model, and separates the wheat from the chaff.

Corporate social responsibility and triple bottom line reporting as means of integrating corporations more cohesively into social environment in which they operate. Counterintuitively, very little crisis communication literature meld the idea of working with corporate social responsibility stakeholders, with the view of solving reputational crises.

Though it may appear this book is all about helping organisations protect their profits and shareholders from crisis, which is not entirely the case, this book provides guiding principles for solving reputational crises of many types and scenarios, through a collaboration of stakeholders, best practice, and focussing on the greater good. Using these principles, this book explores crisis case studies, probes academic research, and questions some of the established practices to develop a more holistic method to deal with any reputational crisis quickly, effectively, and whilst making the world a better place. From Wall Street to interest groups to public relations experts and academics, this book is a valuable resource in achieving better and more holistic outcomes.

Brisbane, QLD, Australia Tom Schermer

Acknowledgements

With thanks,

In part, this book came out of my time as a mature-age student at university, doing PhD but just not buying into the politics within the school. As in every organisation there is a reluctance to change from institutionalised habits (ineffective as they may be), most academics were reluctant to support novel research. Yet, perhaps ironically, the founder of the popular modern stakeholder theory, Professor Edward Freeman, encouraged my idea over social media.

Likely, if it wasn't for my friend Dr Max Newlands at JCU telling me over dinner I should just stop buggering about and write the book, I may not have even started as it is a very large field of study. In the end, I even managed to bother Max for some feedback as the first reviewer.

Without the support of my mother and daughter, this book would not have been possible. Beyond their support, they provided me with great insight into the human condition and outlooks. A couple of close friends seemed to have worked out a schedule to call and ask how the book was going and to push me onwards when it seemed too big a task.

I hope this book spurs you on to be better, and do better things whilst being more considerate of others. It is nothing to succeed without integrity.

How to Use this Book

When in Crisis Skip straight to the crisis pathway and reputational crisis action flow charts to decide how you want to deal with the crisis. Next, using your selection, review the stakeholder maps to give you an idea of how things will appear to your stakeholders. Then go to Chap. 7 – Best Practice Method of Dealing with a Reputational Crisis, and the reputational crisis action flow chart, Fig. 7.7.

Educators and Students The first chapters are academically grounded and referenced, and are summarised at the end of each chapter. The "Thinking Differently" chapter challenges the older stakeholder theory–based crisis communication methods and provides a platform for changing towards to more holistic approach to solving reputational crises, using more recent stakeholder theory and its fundamental principles.

Practitioners A quick study of the closing sections of the second and third chapters which are for academic audiences will provide an overview of the main points. The next two chapters are academic orientated justifications for doing things differently. The remaining chapters provide fresh approaches to solving reputational crises whilst reducing the negative impact and increasing mutually beneficial outcomes for companies and stakeholders alike.

Company Directors and Executives Take the time to read the "Thinking Differently" chapter to prepare for handling the potential crises. Suggest communications and stakeholder managers to read the book and report on their requirements for crisis preparations.

Managers If you are not academically inclined, review the closing sections of the second and third chapters. Then read the fourth chapter and absorb the "Thinking Differently" chapter to get a fresh viewpoint on you can engage with your stakeholders. Subsequent chapters are useful for checking if your communications managers and/or consultants are doing everything they should.

Activists and Interest Groups the second and third chapters are academically orientated and provide more detailed insight into reputational crises. The subsequent chapters can be seen as a guide to how crises evolve, the actors involved, and how stakeholder relationships can escalate reputational crises.

Contents

Part I

1 Introduction: What Is a Reputational Crisis? 3
1.1 First Impressions Do Count 5
1.2 The Problem with Just Using the Right Words 6
1.3 Reputational Crises Explained 7
1.4 Why Reputational Crises Will Continue to Occur 9
1.5 Conclusion 11
Bibliography 11

2 Crisis Communication and Reputation Management 13
2.1 What Is a Reputation? 14
2.2 Introduction to Crisis Communication 16
2.2.1 Characteristics of Reputational Crises 18
2.3 Crisis Lifecycles 20
2.4 Categorising Crises 23
2.5 Image Restoration Strategies (IRS) and Situational Crisis Communication Theory (SCCT) 25
2.5.1 Image Restoration Strategies 26
2.5.2 Situational Crisis Communication Theory 31
2.5.3 Reputational Reservoir 32
2.5.4 Attribution Theory 33
2.6 Case Study Research in Crisis Communication 34
2.7 Share Prices in Crisis 34
2.7.1 Financial Markets Reactions to Reputational Crises 36
2.8 Summary of Reputational Crisis Communication Research 38
2.9 Conclusion 40
Bibliography 41

3 Reputational Crisis Stakeholders – Fluidity in Identities 45
3.1 Without Stakeholders 47
3.2 Stakeholder Theory 47
3.2.1 Freeman's Stakeholder Theory 48
3.2.2 Stakeholder Theory Problems in Crisis Communication 50
3.3 Stakeholder Empathy 50
3.4 Finding the Stakeholders 52
3.5 Stakeholder Conflicts and Allegiances in Reputational Crises 52
3.6 Stakeholder Theory in Traditional and Social Media 53
3.6.1 Stakeholder Theory Complications in Social Media 54
3.6.2 Accountability and Representation in Traditional and Dynamic Social Media 55
3.7 Who Is Important in a Crisis 58
3.8 Summary 65
Bibliography 65

4 Managing Perceptions – Media in Reputational Crises 67
4.1 The Reach of Media 68
4.2 Social Media 69
4.3 Framing and Meaning Makers – History 71
4.3.1 Propaganda for War 71
4.4 Presenting to the Media and Social Psychology 73
4.4.1 In the Media Scrum – Legitimacy Gap Theory 73
4.4.2 Media and Friends – In-Group and Out-Group Behaviours 74
4.4.3 Outsider Losing Control of the Narrative 76
Bibliography 76

Part II

5 Crisis Communication and Management Challenges 81
5.1 Examples of Issues Not Fixed 82
5.2 Obstacles in Stakeholder Theory for Crisis Communication 84
5.3 Obstacles Resulting from Attribution Theory for Crisis Communication 84
5.4 Shortcomings of Crisis Communication Focus 85
5.5 Most Companies Want Free Media, But Not During a Crisis 86
Bibliography 87

6 Thinking Differently: Reputational Crises Resituated 89
6.1 What Is Considered an Offensive Act? 90
6.1.1 Acknowledge That the Act Is Considered Offensive 91
6.1.2 Association with the Offensive Act 91
6.1.3 Why and How to Apologise 92
6.1.4 Is It a Crisis? Are the Crisis and the Target of a Crisis Not the Same Thing? 93

6.2 Viewing Preventative Measures Differently 93
6.3 Making Reparations.. 94
6.4 Summary of Crisis Management Challenges 95
6.5 Fluidity in Dealing with Crises and Conflicting Stakeholder Interests 95
6.5.1 Stakeholder Viewpoints................................ 96
6.5.2 Blame 97
6.6 Developing New Stakeholder Maps 98
6.7 Implied Rules of Conduct 104
6.7.1 Corporate Social Responsibility 104
Bibliography 106

7 Best Practice Method of Dealing with Reputational Crises 107
7.1 Solving a Reputational Crisis 108
7.2 Crisis Panels... 109
7.2.1 Purpose 110
7.2.2 Methodology 111
7.3 Appointing a Crisis Communications Manager 117
7.4 The Crisis Communications Centre......................... 117
7.5 Dealing with Affected or Aggrieved Stakeholders 118
7.6 Crisis Fixed – Ten Steps to Effective Crisis Resolution 119
7.6.1 Summary 126
7.7 Media Statement Templates................................. 126
7.7.1 Initial Media Statement................................ 127
7.7.2 Second Media Statement............................... 129
7.7.3 Social Media and Updates.............................. 130
7.7.4 News Media Organisations 131
7.8 Summary – How to Fix Reputational Crises Whilst Leading the Industry Ethically.......................... 132
7.9 Limitations, Obstacles, and Concerns 133
7.10 Conclusion.. 137
Bibliography 138

8 Crisis Prevention 141
8.1 Managing Stakeholder Relationships 142
8.2 Stakeholder Monitoring...................................... 143
8.3 Media Surveillance 144
8.4 Ethical Data Management 146
8.5 Reputational Crisis Insurance 148
8.6 Summary 148

9 Crisis Preparedness Quiz 149
9.1 Answers to Crisis Preparedness Test........................ 152
Bibliography 157

Index... 159

About the Author

Tom Schermer Spending decades as a business owner and as an agent for various large corporations, I found that helping competing parties find a mutually beneficial solution was the most effective (and profitable) way to resolve disputes. When later studying mass communication (towards journalism qualifications), I noticed that the same conflict occurred between the stakeholders in news stories. With a hobby of investing in shares I saw the potential of reputational crises to impact companies, stakeholders, and shareholders alike.

Taking my approach to resolving conflict with mutually beneficial outcomes, I pursued PhD research in reputational crises. Despite the volumes of literature on reputational crises, at best a few authors hinted at the possibility of changing the way things were done. Unwilling to write a thesis that supported ineffective theories, I put everything I had learned in business, communications, and relationships into this book with the view of overcoming some oversights and obstacles in literature, misnomers in business, and emotionally charged stakeholder groups.

This book uses academic research to set the stage for practical solutions to what are quickly becoming some of the most important conflicts in the history of our species, reputational crises. Even if you can ignore that reputational crises regularly cost corporations more than the Gross Domestic Product of up to eight countries, and that the original stakeholder theory is nearly always read at a superficial level, you cannot afford to ignore that interest groups can now destroy the largest companies through reputational crises. Reputational crises events are also a unique time when the most powerful meet with their accusers, although nearly always in the news media.

This is definitely no longer a world where we can work in isolation. We can expect to have a large impact and at least an equally large responsibility to do the right thing. Reputational crises can and often do force organisations to listen to disaffected stakeholders. Those are times when the interest groups have a tremendous amount of influence over the issues, and immediately affect the well-being of the organisation. Yet, hidden in the chaos of a crisis is often a perfect opportunity to progress an organisation to be bigger and better than before whilst, at the same time, fixing those concerns that brought about the crisis. It is not enough to just do the job when instead you can make the world a better place. Perhaps the biggest single source of problems in the world is people's inability and lack of interest in seeing another person's viewpoint. When it comes to reputational crises, everyone has to listen... there are at least a hundred billion reasons every year to do just that.

List of Figures

Fig. 1.1 The right combination of crisis communications and actions 7

Fig. 2.1 Homogenised model of crisis communication strategies 39

Fig. 3.1 Basic crisis stakeholder map prior to social media........................... 54
Fig. 3.2 Basic crisis stakeholder map since social media 55
Fig. 3.3 Social media stakeholder salience in reputational crises.................. 61

Fig. 6.1 Traditional stakeholder viewpoint – Jeremy Clarkson 99
Fig. 6.2 Thinking differently on stakeholder viewpoint – Jeremy Clarkson 100
Fig. 6.3 Traditional stakeholder viewpoint – BP.. 101
Fig. 6.4 Thinking differently on stakeholder viewpoint – BP...................... 101
Fig. 6.5 Traditional stakeholder viewpoint – Dreamworld 102
Fig. 6.6 Thinking differently on stakeholder viewpoint – Dreamworld 103

Fig. 7.1 Crisis pathways flowchart... 109
Fig. 7.2 Stakeholder centred: Interest group... 114
Fig. 7.3 Stakeholder centred: Media 114
Fig. 7.4 Stakeholder centred: Regulators 114
Fig. 7.5 Organisation centred.. 115
Fig. 7.6 Non-centred crisis panel 115
Fig. 7.7 Reputational crisis action flow chart.. 125

List of Tables

Table 2.1	Image restoration strategies	27
Table 2.2	Image restoration strategies effectiveness continuum	30
Table 2.3	A glimpse of crisis costs	38
Table 3.1	Stakeholders common to reputational crises	58

Part I

This first part of the book explains what reputational crises are, how they are relevant, and how they work. The popular stakeholder theory is unpacked and placed next to its common understanding and usage. The stakeholder chapter gives an overview of common crisis stakeholders, and works towards understanding who is important. Next, media's role in reputational crises is explained and related to stakeholders. The final chapter of this first part focusses on the obstacles in contemporary understandings, knowledge, and actions in reputational crises. This sets the stage for a new and refreshing view on reputational crisis communication and management, as set out in the second part of this book.

Chapter 1
Introduction: What Is a Reputational Crisis?

Abstract This chapter explains in practical terms how reputational crises are everywhere, how they impact our lives, and begins to unpack how reputational crises are most often dealt with. Through doing so, the underlying causes of reputational crises are brought to the forefront and understood as the driving forces of actors in most reputational crises; the obligations of corporate executives to look after shareholder interests, and the roles and motivations of interest groups.

This chapter looks at why reputational crises will continue to occur as the motivations of company executives, news media, politicians, and interest groups, are intrinsic to reputational crises. The common strategy of using apologia and accounts is discussed and found to be incomplete solutions to the problems that cause reputational crises. This chapter signifies the problem of merely communicating reputational crises strategy, finding that communication alone can be counterintuitive to solving and preventing future crises.

The causes of reputational crises and popular reputational crisis strategies are both derivative of stakeholder theory as posited by Freeman. These preliminary findings point to a need more in-depth revision of reputational crises, Freeman's original (1984) stakeholder theory, and Freeman's subsequent revisions of stakeholder theory, to find solutions to reputational crises.

Every single day new reputational crises lead the news headlines, your social media feeds, and conversation at the dinner table. This chapter explains what reputational crises are and how they affect our everyday lives. Reputations are explained and how most people first learn of a reputation when the organisation (or person) is featured in the news media, laying the foundation that doing and saying the right is the only path forward. The extent of the impact of reputational crises is rarely considered but they play a very large part in changing our living, working, and natural environments. Reputational crises have an effect on what we eat, drink, what type of houses we live in, who runs our country, and what is classed as acceptable. In this introduction, the fractious nature of reputational crises is explained, providing an understanding for why reputational crises will continue to dominate news headlines.

T. Schermer, *Reputational Crises Unspun*, https://doi.org/10.1007/978-981-16-5130-4_1

Imagine one of the wealthiest and most influential companies in the world is caught out for doing the wrong thing and it's cost its founder US$72,000,000,000. Some of the company's biggest advertisers and nearly most of its customers are at odds with the company's CEO. Every news channel in the world is covering it. You would be forgiven for thinking that it is not a common occurrence. You would expect that given the amount of money at stake, and the millions of people involved, this situation is unique and won't be allowed to happen again. You would think it is a rarity, and right now you are probably thinking, how did I miss this major piece of news? And which company are we talking about?

The reason you may not know which company it was is because reputational crises happen every single day right across the world. These are the things that fill up newspapers. They are nearly always are mentioned every day in the first 10 min of your television news. They are always listed in your social media feeds, and nearly always are reputational crises the reason for pickets and protests. Politicians love to get involved in reputational crises as it gives them a chance to boast about their own values and thereby increase their political support. Interest groups are created overnight to take on these companies and try to force them to change their ways while in the media spotlights. Often when such changes happen, they are called the David and Goliath battles and company CEO's, directors, and managers are publicly shamed for not coming to their senses sooner. And nearly always, the companies and their stakeholders are seen as adversaries and the interest groups have weakened the reputation of the company. The CEO is often quickly stood down (if for no other reason than being seen as bullied by the media and stakeholders for bad behaviour). Nearly always are reputational crises followed with an exodus of company directors and replacement of most senior management.

The company listed above for wrong doing was once again Facebook. Its founder, Mark Zuckerberg, was caught in the crosshairs of interest groups for not effectively regulating Facebook content by removing hate speech (Sakzewski, 2020). Even the largest social media company could not contain the outcries that came from the Stop Hate for Profit campaign. Only a few months prior there was hardly any mention of Facebook not doing enough to stop hate speech (Hern, 2020). But then the Stop Hate for Profit campaign had not completely managed to get into the spotlight. A number of events, namely the death of a black man by the hands of a police officer in the United States, triggered the social movement storm that eventually caught Mark Zuckerberg, as one of the richest and most influential people in the world, in its crosshairs.

This is not the first reputational crisis for Facebook. The company has been the focus of many reputational crises since its inception. So much so that it can even boast that a movie was made about the way the company originally came up with its social media platform. Perhaps with Facebook having a reputational crisis is somewhat of an irony, as the social media platform is instrumental in many companies, government organisations, NGOs, politicians, celebrities, CEOs, and ordinary people suddenly find themselves the centre of attention and in the midst of a reputational crisis. Social media is continuing to become a bigger part of reputational crises, so perhaps it is only fitting that Facebook leadership is the focus of the occasional reputational crisis.

Calling this particular Facebook reputational crisis a perfect example of what can happen, might be considered short-sighted as Facebook is one of the wealthiest, most powerful, and well-known companies in the world today, and likely you are thinking that this doesn't happen to even the large business, let alone a small business. You would be forgiven for thinking that. Businesses of all sizes become embroiled in reputational crises. The reason for using this Facebook crisis as an example was to illustrate that not even one of the largest and most influential companies in the world can't avoid reputational crises. And reputational crises are common to all types of organisations and all sizes of organisations.

Interestingly, reputational crises are nearly always not understood very well. Interesting, because you would expect that a phenomena that costs companies literally hundreds of billions of dollars per year, would be something that every company executive knows backwards. Most haven't a clue. Hundreds of leaders are dethroned as a direct result of reputational crises every year, amongst its casualties are Prime Ministers, film stars, brilliant leaders of knowledge and sports and arts. Yet public relations companies, business consultants, and scholars keep circling around the same ineffective strategies that have cost their clients everything. This book challenges how reputational crises are understood, how they are studied, and how reputational crises are dealt with. This book offers a refreshing view on how we can deal with others, including how others view us.

1.1 First Impressions Do Count

You only get one chance to make a first impression. Chances are that most of your crisis stakeholders have never heard of your organisation, until the crisis. But then they haven't heard directly from your organisation, but from the media instead. And the media only went with what they thought would draw in lots of readers, viewers, or listeners. This means that the media coverage at the beginning of a reputational crisis is nearly always negative and sensational. And as a rule, the first news media on a reputational crisis will not include any quotes, anecdotes, and will be loose in facts as the news media agent wants to be the first to break the story and doesn't have time to do all the extra work, as the crisis is breaking news.

Putting out a close to perfect first media statement is critical to making a favourable impression to the stakeholders, both new and old stakeholders. If you say and do the right thing, you will gain support during the crisis and likely increase your support base thereafter, be it through new customers, political allies, better suppliers, and so forth. On the other hand, making a bad impression the first time you engage with the crisis in news media, you will practically be forcing the new stakeholders to side with opponents and claimants. These new stakeholders will then instead of being your allies, will be forming an allegiance against your organisation, and in support of your opponents. It is therefore critical to make sure you get your first news media release as close to perfect as possible.

1.2 The Problem with Just Using the Right Words

A lot of crisis communication literature focusses on what are the right words to use to have a favourable response from stakeholders. However, such a strategy fails to take into account a number of factors that contribute to the cause of the crisis. That is, the stakeholders are holding the organisation to account for what is perceived a wrongful action. This type of strategy is not the most conducive to solving the reputational crises because;

- To say the right words but take no action to remedy or prevent similar future events might at best placate a tired stakeholder, but stakeholders who are engaged with the crisis and very concerned might very well use it to escalate the crisis.
- To talk down the importance of crisis stakeholder claims or concerns can often have a negative impact on news media consumers who do at times align themselves with other active stakeholder groups, and thereby escalate the crisis.
- To place the organisation at the centre of the crisis whilst it is the crisis stakeholders that escalated the issue is strategically naïve, as it promotes the negative notion that stakeholders only exist to serve the organisation, and that stakeholders are a secondary concern to the organisation's objectives (which are often objectives of financial gain).
- It is often implied that all crisis communication messages are intended for all stakeholders and a single message will have the same impact on all stakeholders. This implies that all stakeholders can be treated the same, yet in typical reputational crises stakeholder groups are from all creeds and often opposing viewpoints.
- Often in social media strategies, and in particular in the time pressurized conditions that are intrinsic in reputational crises, social media crisis stakeholders are often treated as the same type of stakeholder.

It is clearly not enough to just say the right words in a reputational crisis; you also have to take the right actions. This quickly makes things more complicated as you wrestle to find the right message and the right actions. Any other combination will likely make the crisis worse as illustrated in Fig. 1.1 (see below).

The idea that using the right words will inherently improve the situation and reduce crisis intensity, rarely comes with the warning that it does more harm to say you are going to fix things, and then not do anything. Many reputational crises are centred around honesty and an organisation having done the wrong thing whilst it claimed to be doing the right thing. Thus simply saying you will do something to fix things, and not follow through, will almost guarantee that the crisis will worsen as stakeholders will simply assume you are again saying one thing and doing a different thing. And as reputational crises are about the perceptions of the organisation,

Incorrect words	Correct words	Incorrect action	Correct action	Crisis impact
X		X		Crisis escalated
X			X	Crisis escalated
	X	X		Crisis escalated
	X		X	Crisis reduced

Fig. 1.1 The right combination of crisis communications and actions

doing the right thing and not saying the right, will likely allow the crises to worsen as it will seem that the organisation is not communicating its intentions or actions, and thereby is perceived to be less trustworthy.

The large volumes of research on reputational crises, which includes many historical case studies and laboratory styled studies to gauge audience reactions, spare little to no thought to getting the combination of the correct words and correct actions.

In light of all these obstacles, it might seem nearly impossible to do the right thing in a reputational crisis, and completely impossible to come out of a reputational crisis in a better shape than before the crisis. However that is only if we subscribe to the idea that the best methods have been developed and are already in use. This book questions the methodology of crisis communication studies and supporting literature whilst reviewing the common misuse of stakeholder theory that spawned incomplete ideas that encourages only partly informed crisis managers to take control of a crisis.

1.3 Reputational Crises Explained

Reputational crises are somewhat a mix between scandals and crises. Whereas scandals often relate to specific attributable actions by a person or organisation and do not necessarily mean the person has done something that affects others in a negative way, and crises generally don't attribute its cause to a single person or organisation, reputational crises nearly always affect others in a negative way and are always attributed to a person or an organisation. The common term crisis generally refers to a situation that has come to a critical point and action needs to be taken immediately, or change to a negative direction is imminent. Often the term crisis is used to describe natural disasters and subsequent events. In mainstream media the word crisis is regularly included in a news story to infer urgency. Reputational crises are about a reputation being in crisis, often in a state that is negative and always beyond the normal.

The idea of the reputational crises is that the reputation (which is often generally a good reputation) has reached crisis point by means of media, stakeholders, and of course stakeholder's social media has become focussed on an offending action. So in basic terms, a reputational crisis is a time critical event where a reputation is at stake, and often stakeholders are negatively affected by some kind of offending action.

A lot of people would say who cares? No one cares about an organisation that they don't have any direct dealings with, let alone caring about the reputation of that organisation. And as for stakeholders... well that's just a fancy term to acknowledge the existence of pretty much everybody. It seems too messy, too difficult to be relevant, and not interesting.

But it is through reputational crises that laws are made, often really quickly and as a result, often these laws are very poorly constructed, creating many subsequent problems later. Reputational crises regularly lead to politicians making laws that are just knee jerk reactions. These laws immediately effect organisations and in some hidden ways, they affect your way of life. Sometimes this means that your bank won't approve your loan application because suddenly the government's laws for lending criteria changed overnight. Or the price of your daily bottle of milk went up by 20% overnight. Or your supermarket's fresh baked bread is no longer being made and part baked on the other side of the world and then being shipped your local supermarket (Han, 2014).

In your workplace, reputational crises can do more than just affect the way you do your job, or where do you your job. Many companies shut down permanently as the result of reputational crises, so there is no job at all. In government jobs, a reputational crisis can mean the restructure of entire departments, many job losses and changes in hierarchy and the way everything is done. When an amusement park had a crisis it shut down immediately for months (Kishore, 2016). When your airline has a crisis, its entire fleet of planes may be grounded so you can't fly anywhere (Crowe, 2019). Closer to home, your local mayor mind be worried about the risk of a reputational crisis and start suing people for defamation on social media (Goodenough, 2019). A reputational crisis might just be what is needed to save a local nature reserve from being turned into a high-rise complex (Cannane & Trigger, 2018). Your local member of parliament might stand down from the Parliamentary Ethics Committee because of a reputational crisis (Killoran, 2014). Or more simply, husbands are being told they can't take the family pooch to Dog Obedience classes anymore because the instructor is known to be promiscuous. Or you simply can't buy strawberries that are safe to eat (Williams, 2018; Ogg, 2018).

Looking at the bigger picture, reputational crises change the way the world is run. Reputational crises lead to not only changes in laws, but also the way stakeholders are dealt with. With an ever increasing demand for organisations to become better citizens, there still seems to be a gap between how societies and communities think organisations should act, and how the heads of those organisations think the organisation should act. Corporate social responsible goes a long way to bridging that gap, but the philosophical differences between the two groups are far from being resolved. Society ideally wants everyone to act for the greater good, whereas company executives are legally obligated to look after the financial interests of their shareholders.

Oftentimes reputational crises are exactly what interest groups want to happen with the organisation they are trying to push to change their ways. For instance, an anti-logging interest group would love it if the logging company they are protesting against is being held to account for an offensive action in news and social media. When an organisation is the focus of a reputational crisis, it nearly always gets the attention of politicians, other news media, government regulatory bodies and so forth. Generally reputational crises often quickly result in some form of inquiry to determine who did what, where it went wrong, and who will be blamed. Whilst those enquiries are happening, the entity at the centre of the crisis will have to operate at a reduced capacity until it has been cleared of wrong doing. But rarely do these reputational crises occur without a negative impact on other people or groups. Generally they occur because the entity experiencing the crisis has stepped too far over the line that society finds acceptable. This being the line where there is a lot of grey area both ethically and legally, yet nearly always clearly noticeable within that grey area is a justification by the entity for an action it took, which is clearly wrong in relation to stakeholders or the environment.

1.4 Why Reputational Crises Will Continue to Occur

From one point of view, it could be construed that a reputational crisis can be displayed in a three dimensional model whereby outer nodes represent; the company experiencing the crisis, stakeholders, the media, legislators, and shareholders, and at the centre of it all, human values. This viewpoint allows a reputational crisis to be understood as a problem centred around human values, where the offending action causing the reputational crisis prioritises values that are not congruent with the stakeholders, media, and so forth. Often it seems that this is exactly what happens during a crisis as the news media frame the stories around companies being dishonest, or destroying the environment, or just being plain greedy. Thus it is reasonable to suggest that such a model depicts how there is a conflict between a company and the stakeholders, in terms of how the company values, greed for example, conflicts with the socially acceptable idea that things should be shared so everyone can have some.

Although this viewpoint does explain how the offensiveness of a reputational crisis becomes a contentious point between a company and its stakeholders, it does nothing to offer solutions to reputational crises as the value priorities for an organisation cannot be expected to match those of society, if legally the company exists purely for the benefit of its shareholders. And because corporate officers are legally bound to look after the interests of the company's shareholders, it is likely that reputational crises will continue. Hence a different solution is needed. One where not only the company (and by default its shareholders) benefit, but also where the stakeholders needs are met at least in some part. For if the stakeholder's needs are not going to be met in part and the company continues as it has, it won't be long before another crisis occurs.

If crises don't result in changed behaviour by the organisation, then the crisis is bound to reoccur, and for interest groups this means that the offending behaviour by the company will also reoccur, unless the crisis led to politicians and legislative bodies being involved and forcing the company and its industry to change to avoid such offending acts.

Because of this, most of us living in a modernised western society participate in reputational crises from time to time. We are active members of the community, many people participate in interest groups, and work for large organisation which may take a misstep from time to time. We also consume the news, we are active in social media, and we purchase goods and services from organisations.

However, for many organisations interest groups are often thought of as tertiary stakeholders. That is to say interest groups are not considered to be important enough to be engaged with on a day to day basis. Consequently in reputational crises interest groups often are just an afterthought who at times may be obstacles for the organisation to avoid. For interest groups many large organisations are well beyond the reach for regular interactions and discussions.

For interest groups, large organisations and particularly large companies are seen as immense powerful structures that not only have a lot of wealth, they also have a great amount of resources in terms of connections ranging from great attorneys who can get them out of legal trouble, to political connections that allow them to call the relevant government minister to influence outcomes. Often the sheer volume of administrative and legal staff employed by large companies means it is impossible for an interest group to connect with the right person at a large company to discuss concerns or issues.

This problem for interest groups is evident everywhere. For example; members of interest groups protesting greyhound races for animal liberation are unable to contact the head of the greyhound racing association, much less the commercial sponsors of greyhound racing. In another example, residents protesting to stop a large development on an environmentally protected region rally in the streets, in the news, and online. But none of them are able to get an appointment with the developer or the relevant government administrators or bureaucrats who make decisions.

During recent decades, as a result of research on theories of corporate social responsibility and triple bottom line reporting, some organisations are engaging more with interest groups. However these are often limited to organisations with vast amounts of wealth and extraordinary profits. In those instances some organisations do engage with their interest groups, when the organisation determines that the interest group has a legal legitimacy to be involved. However, such engagements are always likely to result in a favourable outcome for the organisation as the corporate executives are legally bound to look after shareholder interests, even when stakeholder interests are prioritized in news media.

Often when an organisation is covered in the news media for stories, interest groups are consulted by the journalist for contrary viewpoints. For instance, a story about parliamentarians giving themselves a large pay increase will also include some viewpoints from trade union leaders. As a mining company purchases mining rights from the government, traditional land owners and environmental groups will be consulted for the opinion by the journalist for the media coverage. And typically when a finance company announces a big dividend for its shareholders, social welfare groups are welcomed by the media to give their point of view. In each of these examples, which are just a few snapshots of how news media journalists bring in groups as news sources, the interest groups and the organisation are often competing for their viewpoint and interests to be considered more important and socially correct, with the view of gaining support from the readership.

1.5 Conclusion

Reputational crises affect the way we live our lives today, into the future, and how we view the past. The outcomes of these highly mediated events often influence and shape the laws that govern the way we live, the manner in which politicians represent themselves, and how interest groups seek to engage organisations and the public. Reputational crises shape the public perception of organisations from the onset as often people haven't heard of the organisation until it is held to account in the news media for having committed an offending act. Arguably most confounding is that most countries have laws that mandate that company officers look after shareholder interest, even if it is at the cost of society and stakeholders. Crisis communication theory and practice relies heavily on the commonly abbreviated idea of stakeholder theory which places organisations at the centre of everything and everyone else is there to serve the organisation. This means that corporate executives will always be at odds with interest groups. Crisis communication literature, practice, and theorists, have not adapted the use of stakeholder theory to fix and prevent reputational crises.

The following chapters describe the more common and better understandings and obstacles in crisis communication theory and practice, and provide templates for solving these problems, both in theory and in practice.

Bibliography

Cannane, S., & Trigger, R. (2018, December 9). *The developer, the whistleblower and the minister.* Retrieved July 2020, from ABC News – Background briefing: https://www.abc.net.au/news/2018-12-09/the-developer-the-whistleblower-and-the-minister-toondah-harbour/10487806?nw=0

Crowe, A. (2019, July 1). *Regional Express engineers call for grounding of fleet over safety concerns.* Retrieved July 2020, from https://www.dailyliberal.com.au/story/6250273/airline-safety-concerns-regional-express-slams-cowardly-approach/

Goodenough, C. (2019, January 21). *Redland mayor Karen Williams takes legal action on Toondah Harbour video.* Retrieved July 2020, from Redland City Bulletin: https://www.redlandcitybulletin.com.au/story/5862301/mayor-takes-legal-action-on-video/

Han, E. (2014, June 18). *Coles guilty over false 'freshly baked' bread claims.* Retrieved July 2020, from The Sydney Morning Herald: https://www.smh.com.au/business/coles-guilty-over-false-freshly-baked-bread-claims-20140618-3addf.html

Hern, A. (2020, July 1). *Third of advertisers may boycott Facebook in hate speech revolt.* Retrieved July 15, 2020, from The Guardian: https://www.theguardian.com/technology/2020/jun/30/third-of-advertisers-may-boycott-facebook-in-hate-speech-revolt

Killoran, M. (2014, October 26). *Dumped plonker MP Peter Dowling has 'no regrets'.* Retrieved July 2020, from Courier Mail: https://www.couriermail.com.au/news/queensland/dumped-plonker-mp-peter-dowling-has-no-regrets/news-story/4956c2f48a4da0b8b96ac4723eab2a74

Kishore, D. (2016, December 10). *Australia's Dreamworld theme park reopens after fatal accident but witnesses low attendance.* Retrieved July 2020, from International Business Times: https://www.ibtimes.co.uk/australias-dreamworld-theme-park-reopens-after-fatal-accident-witnesses-low-attendance-1595814

Ogg, M. (2018, September 14). *Confidence in crisis: Overcoming collateral damage after strawberry needle disaste.* Retrieved July 2020, from Business News Australia: https://www.businessnewsaus.com.au/articles/confidence-in-crisis%2D%2Dovercoming-collateral-damage-after-strawberry-needle-disaster.html

Sakzewski, E. (2020, June 29). *A Facebook ad boycott has cost Mark Zuckerberg $72 billion. But will it make any difference?* Retrieved July 14, 2020, from ABC News: https://www.abc.net.au/news/2020-06-29/facebook-ad-boycott-costs-zuckerberg-7-billion-what-does-it-mean/12402062

Williams, P. (2018, September 14). *Strawberry needle scare: What you need to know, and what to do if it happens to you.* Retrieved July 2020, from ABC News: https://www.abc.net.au/news/2018-09-14/strawberry-needle-scare-what-you-need-to-know/1024

Chapter 2
Crisis Communication and Reputation Management

Abstract Reputational crises have been studied for many years and various constructs have been developed to understand these better. Amongst the more popular constructs is crisis lifecycle theory which seeks to explain the various stages of reputational crises. Developing communication solutions to reputational crises, Benoit and Coombs have each developed strategies. Benoit's strategy proposes that accounts and apologia provides an effective communication solution, whereas Coombs proposes a methodology to understanding the nature of the crisis to develop a more effective strategy.

However case study research and meta analyses of crisis communication literature often finds that extant communication strategies are not entirely effective as most reputational crises are unique. That is to say most reputational crises have different actors who have almost unique motivation and are almost always uniquely impacted by the reputational crises. A review of the main elements of reputational crises finds that most solutions are incomplete, and suggests that the nature of reputational crisis stakeholders is likely to be more informative and important as a reputational crisis cannot exist without stakeholders. This suggests we may need to understand the stakeholders instead of just making statements to them.

Reputational crises are a construct. That is to say, they are an event that we can understand as phenomena made up of elements. The main elements of reputational crises are; the company at the centre of the crisis, the stakeholders, the media, and how reputational crises work, are reviewed and discussed. These elements of the crises are all essential, for without any of these elements, reputational crises do not exist. This chapter unpacks each of these elements as they are understood in the most popular and well-studied scholarly constructs. First we look at a reputational crisis… what is a crisis really? What is everyone looking at during a crisis? How does a crisis happen? How do reputational crises evolve? These elements are analysed, compared, and then synthesised in practical terms. The main elements of reputational crises are discussed and related to their importance, providing their relevance and background for the following more descriptive chapters.

T. Schermer, *Reputational Crises Unspun*, https://doi.org/10.1007/978-981-16-5130-4_2

Many crisis practitioners believe the ideal way to solve a reputational crisis is to focus on protecting the reputation of the firm. Though in principle this is a good idea, using this as a primary strategy or priority can have the counterintuitive effect of actually destroying the very reputation they are trying to protect. For instance, if the crisis managers always put the firm first, this soon becomes obvious to the crisis stakeholders who already have the media's attention (due to the crisis), and could easily expose this. As a consequence, this furthers escalates the crisis. A real world example is found in the BP Deepwater Horizon oil spill crisis of 2010. At the beginning of the crisis, the then BP CEO Tony Hayward responded to the media by saying "We're sorry for the massive disruption it has caused to their lives. "There is no one who would like this thing over more than I do, I'd like my life back" (Anderson, 2014, p. 98).

Although the CEO (hopefully) was attempting to express that the crisis had also affected him personally and tried to show empathy this way, the media immediately ran with the "I'd like my life back" quote and it caused even more concern for the manner in which BP was handling the crisis and operated as a company in the public and environmental spheres. Crises are mostly about stakeholders, and central to solving a reputational crisis are the crisis stakeholders. For without crisis stakeholders, there is no crisis. This means it is important to get the messages, communications, and priorities right the first time.

This following chapter discusses reputational crises in greater detail, and is followed with a chapter on stakeholders. The stakeholder chapter first engages with the contemporary and popular views on stakeholder theory, before engaging with the revised version of stakeholder theory and its implications. These definitions are examined for use in social media, and are followed with a brief chapter on media. The second half of this book deals with solving crises in a practical manner whilst employing a holistic approach to stakeholders and reputational crises.

2.1 What Is a Reputation?

In a reputational crisis, the identity of a company is often reviewed to understand the context of the offending action, against a background of how the company normally operates. This follows the idea that a company's past actions is likely to impact the severity a crisis will have on the company's reputation. So if a company has a history of environmental blunders and spills, the stakeholders are more likely to view the next spill as negligence and carelessness. Similarly, if a company has a perfect safety record, any mishap is more able to be viewed as an irregular event.

Thus to gain a better understanding of how stakeholders are likely to respond to crisis that a company experiences, it is important to go back to understanding what an organisation's image is. To do this, we have to go back to the fundamentals of what a company and its image are.

The common way of understanding the image of a company, or any type of organisation for that matter, is to look at the sum of its output that is perceptible by the public. For example, if a company is known to make fun advertisements, good reliable cars, healthy foods, and so forth, during a reputational crisis, its image will be that of one which creates useful and reliable goods for the population. This is because the manner in which companies develop these public images is through their actions and managing their media exposure. These are primary elements of a company's image.

However, a company's image is not always exactly what the company really is. The company is far more than the sum of i's activities and outputs. The very idea that a company is an entity is arguable and can be viewed from different perspectives. But that is another topic and to refrain from digressing, the term "organisation" will be used wherever possible.

An organisation is at best, the sum of efforts made by various individuals employed to create output of a specific type. If we consider this more closely and rationally, we come to realise that the collective of individuals representing a company is indeed the sum of many different people. And all these different people have different priorities for themselves, in both their personal and professional lives.

So looking from the ground up, we see many different individuals all with their own personal lives, goals, and ambitions. It is within the context of their jobs, that their efforts are combined to make an output, which too is the sum of their efforts. Albeit homogenised to synthesize the variation in the human values of the individuals.

This from the ground up view then allows us to see how human values, stemming from the employee's private lives, are inherently pivotal to the development of the company image.

Next if we look at what a company is, we can begin to understand just how much of a company's image is little more than a media construct. In other words, if we look at a company and accept that it is nothing more than a few pieces of paper officially registering the company, a collective of people working together for a homogenised output, all in a (often) leased building with leased equipment, leased furniture, and leased plants, it begs the question of what a company actually is. It makes it obvious that the concept of a company has no requirement for a central or physical existence.

For example, if we were to remove and replace the CEO of Virgin airlines, does the company still exist? And then if we change who actually owns the airlines, does the company still exist? The answer to both questions is yes. Then if we remove 50% of the staff and replace them with new staff, the company still exists. Then if we change the business focus of the company from air transport to road transport, the company still exists. After all this, the very elements that we have come to understand are the basic parts for a company, are actually superfluous to the company continuing on with day to day business. There is not a single individual who is a true representative of any company. Neither the CEO nor ground staff. This then raises the questions, what is the company and what is the company's image?

As a real world example, let's look at the international corporate juggernaut IBM (International Business Machines). IBM is a long established company. It was founded in 1911, and was named the computing-tabulating-recording company.

Following some significant growth in the following decades, IBM was a well-established medium sized business based in the United States. Prior to the commencement of World War II, the company worked with the Nazi regime in Germany to establish protocols for tracking and database management of persecutions of Jews, Gypsies, amongst others (Black, 2012). During the Second World War IBM and its subsidiary companies in Europe were instrumental in the tracking and management of prisoners of the Holocaust (Black, 2012). However if we remove what we just read, then IBM is just another corporate giant creating products that are spread throughout the world. Its logo is easily distinguishable, and most of us probably just know as a company that exists, and is neither good nor bad. It is just another company.

The next section introduces the theories and concepts of reputational crises and the prominent theoretical frameworks that have been developed to understand reputational crises and reduce the impact of reputational crises. First an overview of reputational crises is discussed, which is followed with a comparison of the leading crisis lifecycle theories, and is completed with a review of the leading reputational crisis communication theories, and a brief discussion of crisis communication research methods. This chapter provides a background for the contention that crisis communication strategies and messages should be focussed on stakeholders, and that the concerns of crisis stakeholders are centred on the offensiveness of the perceived actions by the organisation experiencing the crisis.

The three most notable contributors to crisis communication methods have jointly dominated the strategies employed by most organisations. These are Benoit, Coombs, and Freeman (although Freeman's work is that of stakeholder theory, it is arguably the most influential). Benoit (1995) pointed the crisis communication community towards what type of messaging is most effective. Coombs' most renowned work focuses on what type of message is most appropriate in a given situation. Whereas Freeman's (1984) work is focussed on the one thing that really matters in crisis communication; that is the stakeholders. This chapter provides a brief overview of Benoit's and Coombs' work, amongst others, and is completed with a proposition that neither contribution provides adequate reputational crisis solutions. Freeman's stakeholder theory is discussed in the stakeholder chapter of this book, as it is most significant and complicated contribution, albeit not specifically intended to be used in crisis communication.

2.2 Introduction to Crisis Communication

A crisis refers to a situation that has become critical, with the potential of resulting in either a negative or positive outcome for stakeholders (Mitroff, 2005; Mitroff & Alpaslan, 2003; Fink, 1986; Ulmer et al., 2007). The impact of a reputational crisis can be far reaching and can cause an increase in legislation affecting company and industry practices (Sabet et al., 2012; Shrivastava et al., 1988; Benoit, 1997). Reputational crises are becoming more frequent (Alpanlan et al., 2009; Mitroff,

1994; Coombs et al., 2010), and the potential for a crisis to occur is considered almost certain (Coombs, 2007; Mitroff & Alpaslan, 2003; Fink, 1986; Lerbinger, 1997). Because of the increasing occurrence, likelihood, and impact of reputational crises, the corporate insurance industry offers protection in the form of reputation risk insurance (Oxford Metrica, 2012)[1]. When a corporation experiences a reputational crisis, it almost always affects stakeholder orientation towards the company (Coombs et al., 2010).

Definitions of a crisis are often influenced by an author's interest in a specific aspect of the field of study. Leading contributor to crisis communication literature, William Benoit (1995), refers to crises in the context of accounts of crises by media, the organisation, and stakeholders, as accounts were Benoit's (1995) area of interest. Similarly, Lerbinger defined a crisis as "an event that brings, or has the potential for bringing, an organisation into disrepute and imperils its future profitability, growth, and possibly its very survival" (Lerbinger, 1997, p. 4); inferring Lerbinger's concern with interest group strategies in corporate public affairs (Lerbinger, 2006). Coombs (2007, pp. 2–3) defines a crisis as "the perception of an unpredictable event that threatens important expectations of stakeholders and can seriously impact an organisation's performance and generate negative outcomes". This association of stakeholders and their expectations indicates Coombs' interest in stakeholder responses to crisis communication. A less stakeholder centric definition is offered by Ulmer et al. (2015). These authors prefer a more generic definition of an organisational crisis; "An organisational crisis is a specific, unexpected, and non-routine event or series of events that create high levels of uncertainty and simultaneously present an organisation with both opportunities for and threats to its high-priority goals" (Ulmer et al., 2015, p. 8). The authors propose that the unexpected nature of a crisis remains, despite improved information managements systems, as crises "exceed planning expectations" (Ulmer et al., 2015, p. 8). Due to advances in information technology and the increasing frequency of crises, crises are becoming less unexpected (Lerbinger, 1997). For instance, scanning news media pertaining to the industry in which an organisation operates has become a popular and effective means of determining which types of crisis are common to the industry, aiding in crisis prevention (Lerbinger, 2006; Ulmer et al., 2015; Regester & Larkin, 2008).

In summary, a crisis is an event that is mostly unexpected to the organisation. Crisis events often result in a significant volume of media coverage, whereby the organisation is held to account for an act deemed offensive to its stakeholders. Reputational crises can impact an organisation's reputation, and subsequently relationships with many stakeholders. Often at the outset of a reputational crisis, not all stakeholders are known or identified by the organisation. Reputational crises can, and often do, result in organisational policy reviews and changes, and government policy and legislative reviews and changes. Fines, organisational restructuring, and the replacement of organisation executives are commonplace in the reputational

[1] For example; BP lost 54% (US$108 billion) in market capital value at the nadir of the Deepwater Horizon crisis (Sabet, Cam, & Heaney, 2012).

crisis aftermath. A variety of these consequences in the aftermath of a reputational crises, often impact the operating procedures and its high priority goals, including company profits.

2.2.1 Characteristics of Reputational Crises

Scholarly literature on crisis communications provides varying views on the defining characteristics of a crisis. Lerbinger (1997) cited Charles Hermann's (1963) principles that in order for a crisis to exist, the following characteristics must be present "(a) Managers must recognise a threat and believe it will hinder high-priority goals; (b) they must recognise the irreparableness and degeneration of a situation if they take no action; and (c) they must be faced with surprise" (Lerbinger, 1997, p. 7). Following Hermann (1963), Lerbinger (1997) distilled crisis characteristics into three elements; suddenness, uncertainty, and time compression. Lerbinger refers to suddenness to describe the sudden occurrence of a crisis, citing events such as terrorist and malevolent acts. The uncertainty of a crisis according to Lerbinger (1997) refers to the unstable and often unknown factors, in the crisis environment. Lerbinger explains time compression as the time constraints placed on managers in a crisis as they seek to manage and minimize adverse impacts on the organisation as quickly as possible. However, as Lerbinger's (1997) description of crisis characteristics is primarily focussed on the time lines and different events of a crisis, it is more suitable for the development of crisis lifecycle theories. For example, the elements of suddenness, uncertainty, and time compression, are relevant to the different stages in crises, and aptly describe the accelerated timeline of a crisis developing. At a prima-facie level, Lerbinger's (1997) crisis characteristics do not focus on the most significant elements of a crisis, such as stakeholders and media. Without media coverage of an event, most people would be unaware of the event (Schultz, 2004), and without stakeholders, a crisis is likely to be nothing more than an event. Suddenness, uncertainty, and time compression do not sufficiently provide for what could be termed as the polarization between the organisation and crisis stakeholders, that nearly always denotes a reputational crisis.

Benoit (1997) provides a more succinct, yet comprehensive description of crisis elements. In developing the concept of 'image restoration strategies', Benoit (1997, p. 178) stated that a reputational attack must comprise of two elements; "i) the accused be held responsible for an action", and "ii) that act is considered offensive". Benoit (1997) points out that the perception of the crisis as held by audiences is of primary importance, and is a condition to both these elements. Benoit's (1997) first element refers to an accused; which infers that a polarisation exists between the organisation and stakeholders in relation to the crisis. This first element also infers that an account of accusation exists regarding an action. Finally, Benoit's (1997) use of the term "responsible" suggests that the organisation is deemed accountable for that action. Benoit's (1997) second condition develops the concept of the action, through requiring the action to be deemed offensive. Benoit (1997) expands on the notion of crisis stakeholders; however Benoit (1997) stopped short of providing a developed concept of offensiveness from a stakeholder's perspective.

Ulmer et al. (2007, p. 8) define the "key components" of a reputational crisis as; unexpected, non-routine, produces uncertainty, threatens high-priority goals. Ulmer et al. (2015) revised this description to include "creates opportunities", and replacing "threatens high-priority goals" with "threat to image, reputation, or high priority goals" (2015, p. 9). Though the notion that a reputational crisis creates opportunities is sometimes referred to scholarly literature, there is a scarcity of literature that evidences opportunity in crisis for the organisation experiencing the crisis. In contrast, Umler et al.'s (2007) references to uncertainty and threats to high priority goals are regular topics in both academic literature and news media pertaining to reputational crises (Fodor & Stowe, 2012; Benoit, 1995; Coombs, 1995; ABC, 2013; Weisman & Chazan, 2010). The uncertainty of crisis refers to the multitude of directions in which a crisis can develop, which can impact high priority goals such as company earnings and consequently the longevity, structure and operations of a company (Fodor & Stowe, 2012; Pincus, 1985). For instance, as a result of BP's leaking oil well in the Gulf of Mexico, the US federal government placed a moratorium on deep sea oil extraction (Sabet et al., 2012). Similarly, the New South Wales state government placed a moratorium on coal seam gas(CSG) extraction plans following accusations that CSG company Metgasco did not adequately engage in community consultation (Nicolls, 2014).

Many scholars refer to reputational crises as unpredictable, sudden, and unexpected. However some reputational crisis literature does recommended scanning news media and other information sources to determine the likelihood and type of crisis a company is most likely to experience (Heath, 1997; Regester & Larkin, 2008). As one of the early contributors to crisis communication literature, Heath suggests that "issue monitoring and analysis shed insight into belief and attitudes held by stakeholding publics that can affect the destiny of an organisation by the way stakes are granted or withheld" (Heath, 1997, p. 82). Companies can often review their past issues to determine likely causes of crises, thereby allowing crisis managers to anticipate future reputational crises. For instance, the BP Deepwater Horizon spill in the Gulf of Mexico was preceded by a multitude of operational and environmental health and safety issues in the company (Lyall, 2010). In addition, BP had received numerous significant fines for previous oil spills and accidents affecting environmental ecosystems (Greenhouse, 2009). Thus BP's operational and crisis managers should have developed plans and strategies for the likelihood of another other spill or industrial accident, on the basis of BP's previous issues. The unexpectedness of a crisis can be significantly reduced through reviewing the company's own history, and reviewing media to identify the issues that other similar companies are experiencing.

The reputational issues Byron Bay Cookies experienced after receiving their Halal Certification could have been anticipated if the company had reviewed the media and food industry for issues related to Halal Certification. Similarly, the issues Metgasco experienced after notifying the public about its gas field exploration plans could have been predicted had the company reviewed the media for issues related to coal seam gas extraction. In addition, reviewing news media for the region indicates a history of environmental social movements and environmental conservatism (ABC, 2010a, b; White, 2019). To summarize, reputational crises develop through an entity being held to account for an offending act.

When that account is made public through media, it often leads to stakeholder's reviewing and/or changing their orientation towards, and relationship with, the entity. Although crises develop rapidly once the offending act is mediated, the type of crisis and the likelihood of a crisis occurring can often be estimated through regular scanning of media relating to the industry in which the entity operates. Crises can, and often do, have a significant impact on the financial well-being of an organisation and its operational procedures, including industry wide changes to policy and legislation. Much crisis communication literature neglects to look at stakeholder impacts, yet without stakeholders there is no crisis.

Crisis management includes various aspects of dealing with crises, including operations, executive decisions, logistics, and so forth. Reputational crisis communication only focusses on the communications of reputational crises, and seeks to effectively manage crisis communications to reduce the negative impact on an organisation (Avery, Lariscy, Kim, & Hocke, 2010; Benoit, 1997; Coombs, 1998). The following section discusses crisis lifecycles by Fink (1986), Mitroff (1994), and Heath (1997) to provide a context based background of reputational crises. This follows with the prominently cited concepts and theories in academic crisis communication literature; focussing on image restoration strategies by Benoit (1995, 1997), and situational crisis communication theory by Coombs (1995). Crisis communication research and literature is often developed from case study based research (Jaques, 2009) and tested with groups of university students (for convenience sampling) (Avery et al., 2010).

2.3 Crisis Lifecycles

Crisis communication theorists and practitioners employ lifecycle theory to separate a crisis into different consequential stages to analyse crises for theoretical and practical purposes. The different stages of crises are denoted by different actions by the media, stakeholders, and company responses. The crisis lifecycle frameworks and theory by Fink (1986), Mitroff (1994), and Heath (1997) are the foremost cited in contemporary literature. The following section reviews and discusses these various frameworks.

The often cited of the early developer of crisis lifecycle theory, Fink (1986), separates a crisis event into four stages; the prodromal stage, the breakout/acute stage, the chronic stage and the resolution stage. Fink (1986) identified the prodromal stage as the stage where evidence of a forthcoming event may be detected. Such evidence may take the form of interest groups or activists opposing an organisation publically, and increasing in member numbers. In what may be termed as an environment crisis, such evidence could take the form of corroding oil pipelines starting to leak. Fink's (1986) prodromal stage is followed by the breakout or acute stage, when the trigger event occurs, or damage has become obvious. For example, at this stage the opposing interest group has developed significant membership or media strategy to become a focal point for the media and politicians. In an environmental crisis example, the oil pipelines have begun to leak and started to develop into a large oil spill. This stage is signalled with high levels of media coverage of the crisis (Fink, 1986). Fink's (1986) third stage is the chronic stage, when the effects are lingering and clean-up has commenced. In this stage the crisis is still receiving media coverage whilst restoration strategies and negotiations are taking place. For example, in the BP Deepwater Horizon oil spill, the impacts of the oil spill were occurring at the same time as impacted stakeholders began to seek reparations. Fink's (1986) final stage, the resolution stage, is evidenced by a clear signal that the crisis is over. In this stage news media coverage of the organisation has diminished to pre-crisis levels, and the most contentious and demanding issues have been resolved to a sustainable situation. In this final stage of the environmental crisis, the oil spill has been cleaned up, reparations have been completed, and regulatory bodies have ceased to be involved.

Mitroff (1994, 2005) developed a crisis lifecycle comprising of five stages, namely; the signal detection stage, the probing and prevention stage, the damage containment stage, the recovery stage, and the learning stage. The concept of signal detection is to use it as a method of scanning for early warning signs (Mitroff, 2005). This first stage of the lifecycle model suggests that a number of events lead to a crisis (Mitroff, 1994). For example, a reputational crisis cannot start with just an offending act, as it needs stakeholders to be aware in order for it to become a reputational crisis. Hence, most crises are the result of a sum of events. These singular events are often visible if a signal detection program is utilised (Mitroff, 2005). Mitroff (2005) suggested that a crisis such as Ford experienced as a result of faulty outsourced parts, would have been successfully limited if a central reporting procedure, such as a signal detection program, had been employed by Ford. In this, a central reporting procedure would have collated all cases regarding faulty parts, and the substantial increase in cases would have signalled a significant issue. The second stage, probing and prevention, occurs at the same time as signal detection (Mitroff, 1994). Mitroff (1994) argues this stage is part of the normal course of business operations as maintenance schedules. Typically these are functions of quality control programs such as an oil company the checking pipelines for leaks, attending to the issues associated with staff (being exhausted from) working too many overtime hours, and so forth. Mitroff's (1994) third stage, damage containment, covers the period when the crisis breaks out and focuses on controlling the impact of the crisis. That is to say; to stop the crisis spreading beyond the original impact area to avoid further impacts on other areas of the organisation and/or environment. Environmental damage control or containment includes methods such as stopping an oil spill from spreading using containment booms, limiting overtime hours of staff involved in the operational management of the crisis, and limiting the impacts on other parts of the organisation (Mitroff, 1994). In a reputational crisis, such actions may include limiting the adverse impact of the crisis on other stakeholders to the organisation. Mitroff's (1994) fourth stage, recovery, is focused on swiftly returning the organisation to a non-crisis situation to avoid further post-damage impacts. Generally, companies would seek to fast forward to this stage as it is focussed on the minimisation of disruption of day to day business activities, or meeting its contractual demands. The sooner an organisation can return to the focus of its day to day ventures, be it large clients or producing large volumes of oil, the sooner the company can return to the situation of returning profits to its owners. The company would be focussed on returning stakeholder relationships to the pre-crisis state. The final stage in Mitroff's (1994) crisis lifecycle is the learning stage, which is concerned with conducting an examination of the crisis event, how it was handled, and responses by stakeholders and crisis impacts. This stage is signalled by the end of the crisis, and focuses on the organisation learning from the crisis, with the objective of improving the management of future crises. Following lifecycle theory, the completion of this stage is followed by the return to the signal and detection stage.

Heath (1997) engaged with less contemporary literature (including Griffin (1952) among others) and drew on a crisis activism lifecycle model used by an American utility company which defined the various stages as (a) vague discontent, (b) politicisation, (c) legislative awareness, (d) regulatory guidelines, and (e) judicial debate (Heath, Strategic issues management: Organizations and public policy challenges, 1997, p. 164). From this Heath developed the concept of an activist based crisis lifecycle model, defining the various stages as "strain (problem recognition), mobilisation, confrontation, negotiation, and resolution" (Heath, 1997, p. 164). Without much adaptation, these stages align with the crisis lifecycle stages as developed by Fink (1986) and Mitroff (1994). In each model, including the activist centred model by Heath (1997), the crisis rapidly develops, and continues as resolution is sought. In each lifecycle model the crisis ceases to exist once resolutions have been developed and completed.

Crisis lifecycle theory was developed to provide scholars and practitioners a better insight into how and when crises occur. A principal objective of crisis lifecycle research and theory is to learn from past crises and develop a concept of the likelihood of a crisis occurring, and how the crisis occurs, with the aim of mitigating crisis impact and how long the crisis lasts. However, often organisations do not learn from crises (Ulmer et al., 2007; Kim et al., 2009), be it their own crisis or a crisis experienced by an industry counterpart. This failure to learn from past crisis may be the result of failing to scan their industry, failing to understand how crises develop, and failing to actively manage the task of crisis scanning and learning[2] (Ulmer et al., 2015; Kim et al., 2009).

The fundamental principles of the various crisis lifecycle models inform that the:

---

[2]After the Deepwater Horizon crisis BP received criticism for using engineers to speak with the press, as the press found it arduous to translate an engineer's language into layman's terms for the press's audiences. Ironically, when BP sought someone to lead their external communications team for their Australian operations two years later, the main educational qualification required was an engineering degree.

- First stage of a crisis should be that of scanning the environment for clues that a might signal a potential crisis.
- Second stage of a crisis lifecycle is generally signalled by a number of stakeholders taking issue with what they perceive as an offensive action by the company.
- The third stage is signalled by rapidly increasing media coverage of the crisis, and sometimes accompanied by a large increase in support for those stakeholders who perceive the company committed an offending act.
- Fourth stage of a crisis is often signalled by a reconciliatory action by the accused company, or a negotiation between the company and the offended stakeholders. During this stage, the media coverage of the crisis may increase or decrease depending on the nature of the negotiations and stakeholders involved.
- Fifth stage of a reputational crisis is generally signalled by a distinct reduction in media coverage, and/or a resolution is reached between stakeholders and the company, and the company's operations have returned to normal.
- The learning stage of crisis should begin at this stage as crisis communicators and executives review the crisis to develop more effective means to deal with a potential future crisis.

The popular format of crisis lifecycle theories, as depicted by Fink (1986), Mitroff (1994), and Heath (1997), suggest that the reconciliation/negotiation stage of crises do not last very long, and are generally equal in longevity compared to other crisis stages. However, in reputational crises where the offending act of the crisis is associated with social activism that relates to ongoing societal debates, this reconciliation/negotiation stage may be protracted when the societal debates are recurring themes in mainstream media. For instance, Halal certification activists appeared to gain more media coverage when these anti-Muslim groups attracted media coverage (SBS News, 2015; Commonwealth of Australia, 2015; Carmody, 2015). Similarly, an environmental pollution crisis may receive increased levels of media every time an adversely affected species is found, linking a company's pollution to the greater environmental protection issue (Australian Marine Conservation Society, 2015).

2.4 Categorising Crises

Crises can be categorised as intentional and unintentional crises (Ulmer et al., 2007). Intentional crises can be understood as crises that result from deliberate acts, such as terrorism, poor risk management, sabotage, unethical leadership, and so forth (Ulmer et al., 2007). Unintentional crisis may be the result of an accident, disease outbreaks, product failure, natural disasters, and the like (Ulmer et al., 2007). Saunders (2004) extended Hoff's (1984) classification that crises can be anticipated, and unanticipated, with developing the notion that unintentional crises can be classified into three categories. Saunders (2004, p. 139) termed these as "1. Acts of nature such as hurricanes, earthquakes, and epidemics; 2. Intentional acts such as product tampering, bomb threats, or hostage taking; and 3. Unintentional events such as explosions, fires, and chemical leaks". Saunders (2004, p. 139) proposed anticipated crises are "characterised by slowly developing conflicts such as labour, unrest, sexual harassment, and product boycotts". These categorisations are helpful for explaining situations around reputational crises; however they do not account for what are arguably the more recurring crises in contemporary media. For instance, Volkswagen's intentional deceit of product emissions output (Hotten, 2015) can simply be described as a dishonest act. Saunder's (2004) categorisation does not account for dishonest acts, and arguably, the Volkswagen reputation crisis did not slowly evolve.

Lerbinger determined there are three classes of crises; "crises of the physical world, crises of the human climate, and crises of management failure" (Lerbinger, 1997, p. 10). In this, Lerbinger (1997) defines crises of the natural world as "earthquakes, tornadoes, landslides, tidal waves, storms of floods that menace life, property, and the environment" (Lerbinger, 1997, p. 10). Lerbinger (1997) defines crises of the human climate as issues that have developed and escalated through "confrontation and malevolence" (Lerbinger, 1997, p. 12). The confrontation crises of the human climate are brought about through the escalation and confrontation of issues by social action groups that seek to influence the manner in which a corporation conducts its business (Lerbinger, 1997). This description by Lerbinger somewhat accounts for crises that have developed through a company being dishonest, such as the Volkswagen emissions reputational crisis. As social media continues to evolve and gain salience, Lerbinger's concepts relating to social action groups is becoming more relevant as numerous crises have developed through social media based action groups (Tench & Jones, 2015; Vromen, 2008; GetUp Australia, 2020).

In developing a theoretical construct detailing proposed communication strategies in reputational crises, Coombs (1995) developed a basic yet extensive categorisation of reputational crises. Coombs (1995) posited that reputational crises can be categorised by three main elements. These being; locus, stability, and controllability; whereby locus refers to the crisis cause being external or internal to the organisation, stability refers to the crisis history of the organisation, and controllability refers to the crisis cause was within the control of the organisation. Coombs' categorisation allows for a broad description to be represented in each category. However due to the very broad nature of the categories, Coombs' (1995) construct doesn't appear to encapsulate the intentional and unintentional categories as offered by Ulmer et al. (2007), nor the anticipated and unanticipated categories offered by Saunders (2004).

Crisis categorisations are developed to aid with the selection of crisis communication strategies, with the objective of ending the crisis, or at least reducing the offensiveness of the crisis. Although crisis communication strategies are numerous, it is difficult to develop a categorisation that accommodates every type of crisis scenario (Coombs, 1998). For instance, the Byron Bay Cookies Halal Certification crisis can be identified using Coombs (1995) categories; where the locus is internal as the decision for Halal certification was made by the company, the stability of the company indicates that Byron Bay Cookies were not prone to crises, and the controllability measure of the crisis suggests that the crisis causing act was controllable. Ulmer et al. (2007) would classify the crisis causing act as intentional, and using Saunder's (2004) categories, Byron Bay Cookies should have been able to anticipate the crisis. Combining these various categorising methods allows for the development of a more holistic description of a crisis's characteristics. However, the method of employing multiple categorisations would not be practical for practicing crisis managers who are seeking to end the crisis as soon as possible to reduce negative impacts on their organisation. The objective of categorising crises is to develop a suitable crisis communication strategy and the final objective is to limit the negative impact and end the crisis. Applying multiple categorisations becomes elongated and methodologically impractical in time critical crisis situations.

As crisis communication research is primarily focussed on developing stakeholder communication strategies to mitigate the impact of "offensive" (Benoit, 1997, p. 178) acts, the development of a more direct strategy of determining what crisis stakeholders consider offensive, and then developing a communication strategy to address the offensive element, could be a more direct route to the same objective. Reviewing stakeholder theory provides better insight to achieve this.

2.5 Image Restoration Strategies (IRS) and Situational Crisis Communication Theory (SCCT)

Predominantly reputational crisis research is focussed on case studies (Jaques, 2009) and developing effective communication strategies and messages to limit the impact of crises on companies (Avery et al., 2010). The next section is a review and discussion of crisis communication strategies and messages that seek to mitigate crisis impacts, and is followed with a brief discussion of crisis communication research methods.

Contemporary scholarly crisis communication literature focusses on the effectiveness of crisis communication messages and strategies with audiences (Avery et al., 2010). How crisis audiences view not only the crisis communication messages, but also the offensiveness aspect of the crisis is salient to developing effective crisis communication strategies. The foremost cited authors in contemporary crisis communication literature, Timothy Coombs and William Benoit, focussed on communication strategies that aim to reduce or limit the negative impact that crises can have on an organisation's image (Avery et al., 2010). Determining the specifics of the accusations, or "attacks and complaints" (Benoit, 1997, p. 178) central to the reputational crisis, with the aim of developing an effective crisis communication strategy and messages is the cornerstone of Benoit's *image restoration strategies* (Benoit, 1995, 1997; Benoit & Drew, 1997) and Coombs' *situational crisis communication theory* (SCCT) (Coombs, 1995, 1998). Situational crisis communication theory was developed on the basis that in order to understand which type of message must would be most effective in reducing crisis impact, it is necessary to understand the type of accusation that is made against the organisation experiencing the reputational crisis. In other words, the fundamental principle of Situational Crisis communication Theory is determine what specifically of the act leading to the crisis is considered offensive. On determining what the offensive act is, an image restoration strategy (Benoit, 1997) or situational crisis communication strategy (Coombs, 1998) is selected and developed to end the crisis.

2.5.1 *Image Restoration Strategies*

Benoit published *Accounts, excuses, apologies: A theory of image restoration strategies* (1995), in which Benoit used case studies to exemplify and develop the principle of using apologia in crisis communication efforts to reduce the impacts of reputational crises on organisations. Benoit (1997) developed a typology of image restoration strategies linking different types of apologia and accounts to specific types of reputational crises. Image restoration is designed to return the image of an organisation to its pre-crisis state as soon as possible. Benoit (1997) developed fourteen image restorations strategies (Table 2.1 below) that are represented by five catagories; denial, evasion of responsibility, reducing offensiveness of event, corrective action, and mortification (Benoit, 1997).

2.5.1.1 Dealing with Offensiveness – Benoit's Image Restoration Strategies and Critique

Simple Denial Critique

Benoit & Drew (1997, p. 155) explain denial is used similarly to refusal, "One may also shift the blame for the offensive act from self to another person, claiming that he or she performed the act". The notion of refusal as an interpretation of denial is apt in crises, for if someone denies their responsibility, they are in as much refusing to take ownership of the act, its subsequent outcomes, and responsibility for the act.

Both historical case study research and controlled lab styled research shows that simple denial is one of the least effective means of dealing with a reputational crisis. It doesn't matter if the staff, the board, or the CEO believes that the company was not at fault. What matters is what the news media report, and consequentially what the public believes to be true. If the public believes the company was at fault, no amount of denying it is going to change that. This would be similar to a parent addressing a four year old child for behaving badly and the child saying that he/she didn't behave badly. The parent believes that the child behaved badly and that the parent knows better than the child. For a CEO to state to be media that "we didn't do the wrong thing" is similar to the four year old child saying "I didn't do the wrong thing". The public, like the parent, acts like a judge. It is not up to the four year old child to judge him/herself. It is not up to the company or CEO to judge him

Table 2.1 Image restoration strategies

Benoit (1995) strategy	Benoit (1995) key characteristic	Examples
Denial		
Simple denial	Did not perform act	*We didn't do it*
Shift the blame	Act performed by another	*Someone else is to blame*
Evasion of responsibility		
Provocation	Responded to the act of another	*Given the circumstances, we were provoked to do it*
Defeasibility	Lack of information or ability	*We were not made aware of the circumstances*
Accident	Act was a mishap	*It was completely unintended*
Good intentions	Mean well in the act	*We tried to change the situation*
Reducing offensiveness of event		
Bolstering	Stress good traits	*We are doing a great job in fixing the problem*
Minimization	Act not serious	*The damage was only small*
Differentiation	Act less offensive	*What we did isn't as bad as ...*
Transcendence	More important considerations	*It was for a greater good*
Attack accuser	Reduce credibility of accuser	*We stand accused by a liar*
Compensation	Reimburse victim	*We will pay for damages and pain*
Corrective action	Plan to solve or prevent problem	*We are/will fix the leak*
Mortification	Apologise for the act	*We are sorry and* regret *what has happened*

After Benoit (1997, p. 179)

or herself. The public must be allowed to be the judge. It is the company representative's role to facilitate that judgement and make sure that the outcome is more favourable than less favourable. This is not to say that the company should go out of their way to justify their actions, but instead make those actions understood in terms of what society finds important.

Denial or refusal as an image restoration strategy would like cause crisis stakeholders to become more offended, if no other reason than that it infers that the crisis stakeholder is wrong in their attribution of the offending act, and the strategy is at best combative, if not insulting.

2.5.1.2 Evade Responsibility

Under this category, Benoit & Drew (1997) list provocation, defeasibility, accident, and good intentions. Similarly to the denial category, these image restoration strategies are used to deny responsibility through re-attributing the offending act. However in this category, the blame is somewhat carried by the offending actor, but the blame is passed through to attribute it to another cause. In the provocation strategy, the other cause would likely be another actor forcing them to commit the offending act. 'Defeasibility' is used to describe "a lack of information or control over events" (Benoit & Drew, 1997, p. 156). In other words, to attribute blame to the cause which lead to the offensive act, and thereby not take all responsibility for the offending act. Oftentimes 'accident' is used in crisis communication rhetoric (as it was in the BP Deepwater Horizon crisis), as a means to relocate the cause of the offending act away from the company, as a means of intending to save the company's reputation. Benoit & Drew (1997, p. 156) do not offer any examples of 'good intentions' as the last image restoration strategy in the "evade responsibility for event" act, other than saying that good intentions seek to reduce the offensiveness through associating the act with what was a more ethical objective. And thus is more forgivable. Arguably this last strategy is more about reducing the offensiveness of the act.

In crisis communications this category of strategies often does, and is likely to, inflame the offended stakeholders in a crisis, because similar to denial, these strategies seek to reorientate the offended stakeholder to what the organisation believes. But in a reputational crisis the blame has already been attributed to the organisation, and trying to reduce offensiveness or association with the offending act is often seen as combative. This is counterintuitive because the crisis stakeholders have already made up their mind, and will become more incensed by what could be viewed by stakeholders as an argumentative strategy.

2.5.1.3 Reduce Offensiveness

Benoit & Drew's (1997) third category lists bolstering, minimization, differentiation, transcendence, attack accuser, and compensation. Largely this category of strategies does not seek to distance the actor from the blame for the offending act. Bolstering is often used by organisations to remind the audience that the organisation has an excellent track record. Coombs (1995) uses the concept of stability to develop an image, whereby the organisation's past performance is brought into account, creating the idea that the offending act is an anomaly in the organisation's otherwise good behaviour record. Minimization means reducing the negative impact of the offending act, thereby minimizing "the perceived offensiveness" (Benoit & Drew, 1997, p. 156). The differentiation strategy uses "a wrongful act from other less desirable, but similar actions" (Benoit & Drew, 1997, p. 156). Benoit & Drew's (1997) use of transcendence borrows from spiritual transcendence whereby a more elevated position allows one to see things more objectively, citing "attempting to place the act in a larger, more desirable context" (Benoit & Drew, 1997, p. 156). This strategy will only work if the accusers share the belief that the offending act was more desirable than the alternative outcome, and that there was no other means to resolving the situation. Often crisis stakeholders will be quick to offer alternatives that the organisation either did not realise existed, or considered them not suitable. In the case of the latter, the crisis stakeholders are likely to disagree, leading the crises rhetoric down a path of ethical arguments. This is counterproductive as the first objective of crisis communications is to resolve the crisis, rather than prolong a crisis through arguments. “It is possible to attack one’s accuser, suggesting that the victim deserved what happened to them, to lessen the impact” (Benoit & Drew, 1997, p. 156). This strategy may work on the very rare occasion that crisis stakeholders do not have any association or empathy with the accuser, however this is rarely the case as in most crises nearly all stakeholders are nearly always in agreement that the organisation has committed an offending act. This is probably the most risky strategy because if there is empathy for the accuser, then all stakeholders will immediately be inflamed through the adding to the offensiveness with an accusation of dishonesty. Benoit and Drew (1997, p. 156) suggest compensation “to help offset negative feelings associated with a wrongful act”.

2.5.1.4 Corrective Action

Benoit and Drew (1997, p. 156) place corrective action as an independent category and its own image restoration strategy. They posit “the speaker may offer to repair existing damages and/or to take steps to prevent reoccurrence of the offensive act”. The authors list corrective action separate to compensation which in this context makes compensation seem more like a financial offering to forget about the offensive act. Consequently corrective action than is more about offering something to ‘make good’ on damages to affected stakeholders. Offering replacement of affected things with a focus on what the stakeholder/s values may yield a better response as it shows empathy through the display of shared values. This is one of the most effective strategies, if done with a healthy and insightful empathic concern for loss. For affected stakeholders and those concerned with a repeat of the offensive action, the prevention of recurrence may also allow for the stakeholders to infer a degree of empathy.

2.5.1.5 Mortification

This image restoration strategy is the least adversarial of the Benoit’s (1997) typology. Benoit and Drew (1997, p. 156) posit “mortification may include expression of regret (for one’s role in the offensive act, or for the consequences of the act, or both), and request for forgiveness”. Most often during reputational crises an organisation’s legal team will strongly advise against mortification as it could be implied that the organisation is taking responsibility for the consequences of the offensive act, and thereby admit legal liability for the damages incurred, and the admission of guilt may be construed as pleading guilty to possible fines and further legal consequences. However it is possible to express sympathy and regret for undesirable consequences that resulted without admitting legal liability. For example, “we sincere sympathise for the affected stakeholders and regret any suffering they have experienced”, (leaving out terms such as “as a result of the [offending act]” may remove the admission of guilt which the legal teams are concerned with. It is certainly effective to show empathy for stakeholders and remorse for their suffering, without referring to the offensive act, even if a legal debate regarding liability may take place in a courtroom at a later date.

2.5.1.6 Effectiveness of Image Restoration Strategies

Benoit and Drew (1997) tested the effectiveness and appropriateness of the image restoration strategies with students using pre-scripted messages. However the appropriateness of crisis communication strategies is arguably negligible as the nuances of crises and crisis stakeholders are undefinable, broad, and unlimited.

In terms of effectiveness of Benoit's (1997) image restoration strategies, there was a significant degree of variance, as demonstrated in the continuum below (developed from the results of Benoit and Drew's (1997) testing. Mortification and corrective action were found most effective in minimizing and restoring image. Compensation, accident, transcendence, good intentions, defeasibility, shift blame and attack accuser were found to be less effective. Denial, provocation, minimization and bolstering were reported as least affective (Benoit & Drew, 1997). Both the image restoration strategies and their effectiveness are regularly cited, and tested, in academic crisis communication literature (Avery et al., 2010) (Table 2.2).

Image restoration strategies are widely referred to in crisis communication research and often applied in practice. They are effective in establishing a platform for communications with crisis stakeholders, in that they provide a guide for practitioners to follow in the event of a crisis. However, image restoration strategies and messages mostly do not focus on what stakeholders find offensive about a reputational crisis. Instead image restoration strategies are more a generic format for

Table 2.2 Image restoration strategies effectiveness continuum

Most effective
Mortification
Corrective action
Compensation
Accident
Good intentions
Transcendence
Defeasibility
Shift blame
Attack accuser
Differentiation
Simple denial
Provocation
Minimisation
Bolstering
Least effective

After Benoit and Drew (1997)

messages, which could be effective if they address the perceived offensiveness of crises.

2.5.2 Situational Crisis Communication Theory

Leading author in reputational crisis communication, Timothy Coombs (1995), proposed situational crisis communication theory (SCCT). Coombs (1995) suggested that a typology of crisis types would be effective in helping determine the most suitable crisis communication messages. To develop situational crisis attribution theory, Coombs (1995) used attribution theory to categorise the various aspects of reputational crises. In this Coombs employed attribution theory in reputational crises as a means to determine how "people make judgements about the causes of events based upon the dimensions of locus, stability and controllability" (Coombs, 1995, p. 448).

- Locus is employed to determine if the cause of the crisis as internal or external to the organisation,
- Stability is employed to determine if the cause of the crisis event is a regular occurence the organisation,
- Controllability is employed to determine if the cause of the crisis is within the organisation's control (Coombs, 1995).

Coombs (1995) contextualised these dimensions of attribution in crisis communication strategies, and developed flowcharts to assist crisis communicators to determine the most suitable message for a specific crisis. The intent of the flowcharts is that crisis communicators can quickly ascertain the specifics of certain elements of the crisis, and on the basis of those elements the flowchart is used to determine the most effective crisis communication strategy. The elements on Coombs' (1995) flowcharts are; crisis type, evidence, damage, victim status, and performance history. However, "as the crisis milieu is too complex to factor in and to control all variables" (Coombs, 1995, p. 471), it is difficult to develop an exhaustive typology of reputational crisis types and appropriate messages for each type. That is to say, there are so many varying elements of crises that it is difficult to determine what the right thing is to communicate for each particular scenario (Coombs, 1995). Despite this, the situational crisis communication flowcharts are useful, both in aiding the crisis manager in determining the specifics of a crisis, and developing at least a conceptual crisis communication strategy.

Due to the problem of not being able to identify every type of reputational crisis and crisis appropriate message (Coombs, 1995), a volume of literature has been developed using a case by case basis; assessing single communication strategies in specific context scenarios. Consequently for crisis communication practitioners the research outcomes are difficult to apply as most are context specific. Furthermore, the large volumes of literature make it difficult for crisis communicators to quickly assess and identify the research outcomes relevant to their specific crisis, in pressurized time limitations (which are a hallmark of reputational crises).

Coombs' (1995, 1998) contribution to the literature with situational crisis communication theory is significant in that it provides a generic framework useful for the categorisation of crises. The elements of locus, stability, and control, can be applied to any reputational crisis, in theory and practice.

Towards understanding offensiveness both Benoit's (1997) image restoration strategies and Coombs' (1995) situational crisis communication theory are useful in developing crisis communication strategies. Image restoration strategies and situational crisis communication theory are premised on how the audience of the communication strategies perceive the crisis, as opposed to how the crisis is perceived by the news media, or how the organisation experiencing the crisis perceives the crisis. That is to say, the implimentaton of image restoration strategies and situational crisis communication strategies are premised on what is perceived to be the audience's perspective of the crisis. Although the academic literature on crisis communications is rich with information on which types of messages are most effective as strategies, little focus has been given to why these strategies are most effective. It appears the literature would be more complete if research focussed on determining specifically what stakeholders find offensive about a crisis, to allow the organisation to determine the most effective communication strategy to address the perceived offensiveness.

2.5.3 Reputational Reservoir

Coombs (1995) referred to stability, when discussing the past performance of the organisation experiencing the crisis. The notion of stability, or organisational history, is related to what is sometimes termed as reputational reservoir. This infers that the strength of an organisation's reputation is developed over time. Thus when a reputational crisis occurs, an organisation with a strong reputational reservoir can withstand the crisis impacts more than an organisation with a weak reputational reservior. An example of this is BP, which had a recurring theme in its operational history of environmental and workplace health and safety issues (Lyall, 2010), was held to account by stakeholders for not managing known risks. If BP had a reputation of good environmental and operational health and safety performance, the company would likely have been held to account for an accident, instead of malfeasance.

2.5.4 Attribution Theory

Jorgensen (1996) developed a more direct approach to crisis communication audiences and their responses through employing attribution theory to determine to what extent an organisation would be held to account by consumers for behaviour. Specifically, Jorgensen sought to understand the "interrelationship among consumers' cognitive, attitudinal, and behavioural reactions to an organisation in crisis" (1996, p. 346). Weiner's (1986) attribution theory allowed Jorgensen (1996) to rely on the association between the company's communication in a reputational crisis and the consumer's response to the company experiencing the crisis. Jorgensen found that "the stated likely cause of an incident is found to have a more profound effect ...than does company response" (1996, p. 346). Jorgensen's research suggests that stakeholders' responses to reputational crises, can be directly associated to the reported accounts of those crisis. Unfortunately, Jorgensen's (1996) research stopped short of seeking to understand why those accounts influenced stakeholder's behavioural responses to reputational crises. McDonald et al. (2010) employed Jorgensen's (1996) work and included crisis causes and response strategies in their research. This format in part follows the situational crisis communication theory (Coombs, 1995) focus on crisis typology. Their research produced counterintuitive results to contemporary crisis communication literature; a no-response strategy was not as detrimental to the company's reputation as some crisis communication messages (McDonald et al., 2010). In summary, Jorgensen's (1996) attribution theory based research adds to the research significantly through seeking to determine why stakeholders find crises offensive. Jorgensen's (1996) method of applying attribution theory is unique in drawing a more direct route between effective communication strategies and stakeholder responses. For example, most research focusses on if something is well received by stakeholders, and pays little or no attention to what the crisis stakeholders want to hear, or why they want to hear it.

Heath (1997, p. 167) denotes the position of the activist groups in reputational crises (during the strain stage) as "groups create a sense of strain by showing how business actions violate the self-interest of segments of the population". This depiction aptly demonstrates the offensiveness of an act that leads to a reputational crisis as described by Benoit (1997). Despite the utterances by Heath (1997) and Benoit (1997), only a nominal amount of crisis communication research has focused on describing the offensiveness or violations as perceived by social activists or other stakeholders. It is counterintuitive to develop crisis communication messages and strategies to reduce the impacts of a crisis, when resolving the issue with stakeholders through resolution of the crisis is the primary objective. Chapters five and onwards seek to address gaps in the literature by means of suggesting engaging with crisis stakeholders to determine what they consider offensive about crises.

2.6 Case Study Research in Crisis Communication

Crisis communication research literature is largely focussed on the two areas of image restoration strategies and situational crisis communication theory (Avery et al., 2010). The literature is largely represented by (a) controlled experiments with selected participants, and (b) post crises case study analysis. There are however a number of limitations with these research methods. For instance, the testing of the effectiveness of the crisis messages in controlled experiments with selected participants might not always include the variety of stakeholders as often present with a crisis. More importantly, during actual crises, stakeholders are offended and at the time likely aggrieved due to the offending act, and these conditions cannot be completely replicated in the laboratory styled conditions as used in most clinical studies.

Different messages may be more effective with some stakeholders than with others (Benoit, 1997). Post crisis case study analysis are generally an accepted means of studying the effectiveness of crisis communication strategies as case studies mostly take into account the varying influences, factors and environment (Yin, 1993). However, as Jaques (2009) stated, the nuances of case study methodology make the findings of case study based research very context specific. Applying case study results that demonstrate effective crisis communication strategies without replicating the context specific environmental factors often means that the effectiveness of those strategies will be significantly altered. Although these the two main methodologies in crisis communication research contribute to the field, they may prove to reduce the effectiveness of crisis communication strategies as they (a) develop a body of literature that is too voluminous due to the context specific nature of the research (Coombs, 1998), or (b) the application of case study based research if it is applied to a crisis in which not all influences, factors, and environments are the same (Jaques, 2009).

2.7 Share Prices in Crisis

At the core of every reputational crisis is an offensive act, or at the very least a wrong-doing. Often these are met with consumer and regulator backlash and a reduction in company share price. Because the "offensive act" or "wrong doing" is readily understood as something that goes against what we deem to be appropriate behaviour in society, it is natural to think that the worse the offending act of wrongdoing is, in terms of ethics and society, the worse the impact should be on the company, and consequently its share price.

Following the ideal that the company share price should drop as a type of punitive market response, i set about to determine if Benoit and Drew's (1997) study that determined the effectiveness of crisis responses held true to share market responses to media statements. The BP Deepwater Horizon oil spill crisis in the Gulf of Mexico was selected because the crisis was active for approximately half a year and many media statements were released by BP. The second reason for selecting BP for this study was that the company's share price dropped by fifty-eight percent at its nadir, meaning the company's value dropped by US$108,000,000,000. All the media statements made by BP were downloaded, analysed, and categorised to the most fitting of Benoit and Drew's (1997) typology of crisis responses. These types of responses were then matched to share price fluctuations at and after the time of the media releases. The evidence conclusively indicated that the crisis communication effectiveness findings by Benoit and Drew (1997) had no determinable effect on share price fluctuations. In simpler words, the company's statements seemed to have no effect on share price changes. Whether the company had made a statement that expressed remorse or suggested compensation payments would be made, or that the problem was soon to be solved, had no noticeable impact on the share price. Because we are (mostly) led to believe that saying the right thing will lead to being treated more favourably, this result seemed counterintuitive.

The reason for this is that the company's share price is mostly dependent on the profitability of the company. The next section discusses how reputational crises can and do impact the financial wellbeing and viability of companies.

For most companies a reputational crisis is still about dollars and cents because a reputational crisis can have a truly devastating effect on the company's interim profits, the company's capital worth, and a significant enough reputational crisis can easily put a company out of business.

The most common financial impacts reputational crises have on organisations are fines, reduced revenue, reduced profitability, and as a consequence of any of those, a significant reduction in share price if the company is listed on a stock exchange.

Fines imposed on companies, as a result of reputational crises, can have a significant impact on the company's ability to conduct business as the financial penalties may force a company to sell assets that it uses to produce revenue, to pay its fines. Some of the largest fines imposed on companies are: BP – US$ 20,800 million plus US$ 65,000 million compensation, Bank of America – US$ 16,650 million, Volkswagen – US$17,700 million.

The financial impacts of reputational crises are often not limited to fines. Oftentimes when the company's offending act was upsetting to enough members of the public, politicians tend to (increase publicity for themselves and) introduce new legislation that governs how companies operate in those environments. For example, if a mining company was held to account for polluting environmental waterways with its toxic water waste, the authorities would immediately fine the company. But at the same time, the environmentalist lobby groups would have ensured that the event was brought to the attention of mainstream news media, and quickly the public outrage brings it to the attention of a politician. The politician will then often push for legislation to increase environmental safety controls on the company, and in this example, force the mining companies to install more extensive filtration equipment to clean its waste. Without such measures increasing the amount of revenue the company makes, the increase in operating costs would reduce the profitability of the mining operations. Not just for that single site that was the focus of the crisis, but right across all its operations.

Reputational crises often reduce the revenues of the company experiencing the crisis. Very often consumers will boycott a company and refuse to purchase its products or services if it was found to be guilty of wrongdoing. A straightforward example is when a video became popular on the internet of a pizza company employee doing very unsavoury and unhygienic things to customer's pizzas. This immediately led to a massive loss in customers. Less obvious examples would include large home building companies boycotting specific supplies of a large hardware store because its wall bracing ply is directly sourced from Amazonian rainforests and sent to the other side of the world, because with shipping costs included, it was still more profitable for the hardware company to sell the product. Although it may seem that businesses boycotting other businesses seems unlikely, and will not likely have an impact, it does happen often enough, and can have a serious impact on those companies. For instance, when Facebook and its founder Mark Zuckerberg, were caught in the crosshairs of interest groups for not effectively regulating Facebook content by removing hate speech (Sakzewski, 2020) large global companies cancelled their advertising contracts costing Facebook billions of dollars (Hern, 2020). These different types of boycotts can have significant impacts on businesses, and can affect businesses that do not deal directly with the public.

Though some fines and compensation payments may be enough to put some companies out of business, a combination of fines, reduction in revenue, and customer and supplier boycotts can easily risk any company's longevity.

2.7.1 Financial Markets Reactions to Reputational Crises

Reputational crises often do affect company share prices, and very often decrease share price and profitability. For corporate executives this is a problem. Corporate executives are duty bound, and in most western countries legally bound, to look after the company's interests, and so by proxy look after the shareholder's interests.

Shareholder's interests are mostly simple to synthesise; the company should operate at a level that returns dividends (shareholder profit payments) that are equal to or greater than the previous dividends, and the company share price (the shareholder's capital investment) should grow in value. These are the basic premise of any company share investments made by individual investors and institutional investors (institutional investors can be superannuation funds investing into shares, companies buying share of another company, government investments, and so forth).

The investors of shares purchase shares to make money. When a company makes a profit during a year, it pays its owners (the shareholders) the profits. The greater percentage of ownership you have, the greater the percentage of profits you will receive. The share price of a company is mostly determined by its likelihood to pay its owners, the shareholders. These payments are called dividends. Without getting into too much detail, the amount of the dividend payment is calculated as follows:

$$\text{Dividend} = \frac{\text{Total profits of trading period}}{\text{Total number of shares outstanding}}$$

The company share price (what it costs to buy a company share) is based on how much the company dividends are. For example, if you own a company share at $100 per share, and the dividend payment is $8 per year, but another company's shares costs $50 per share, and they also pay a dividend of $8 per year, you would sell your $100 share, buy two $50 shares, and double your return on investment to $16 per share. Which then leads other people to sell their shares in the original company to do the same thing, and the oversupply of those shares will reduce their value until their return on investment (dividends per share) is equal to that of other companies. In other words, if your company's profitability drops, so will its share price. And as reputational crises can affect a company's profitability, share investors (often institutional investors with a large volume of resources to calculate crisis impacts) will attempt to determine exactly how much the company's profitability will be affected by a crisis, and lower what they believe the company's share price to be worth, based on the likely dividends. In those calculations they attempt to determine how much the fines will cost the company, if trade restrictions will likely be placed on the company, and all factors that influence the likely future revenues of the company, including boycotts. Often when a company's reputational crisis is featured in mainstream news, the company's share price will very quickly reduce as a response to those likely impacts on the financial viability of the company.

It is not uncommon for company share prices to drop by 10 to 50 percent as the result of a reputational crisis. These drops can occur as the result of numerous consistent decreases over a longer period, but just as often a company share price drops by 20 per cent overnight as the result of a reputational crisis.

The table below list only a few examples of how much reputational crises can cost companies, and is only a tiny snapshot of the financial ramifications of reputational crises (it was tempting to list every major crisis showing how badly handled reputational crises cost companies trillions of dollars). Every day, on every news channel, every newspaper and news website, yet another crisis is handled badly. It makes it seem as though CEOs and Boards of Directors put very little effort into protecting company reputations (Table 2.3).

The post crisis share price recovery will not happen in a vacuum. That is to say that the company share price will only increase if there is a reason for it to increase, and post crisis share price increases are only going to occur if the company's financial position improves and its revenues return to normal. Financial market responses to reputational crises seem conservative as the share price changes are the result of calculations of the financial impact on the company experiencing the crisis. The most effective way to reduce the financial impacts of a reputational crisis is to deal with the stakeholders and fix the crisis.

Table 2.3 A glimpse of crisis costs

Year	Company	Negative impact on company market capitalisation Market cap. (US$)	Source
2010	BP	108,000,000,000	Sabet et al. (2012)
2016	Wells Fargo	23,300,000,000	Allen (2017)
2018	Facebook	26,500,000,000	Rodriguez (2018)
2018	Facebook	36,000,000,000	Rodriguez (2018)
2018	Facebook	23,000,000,000	Rodriguez (2018)
2018	Facebook	18,000,000,000	Rodriguez (2018)
2018	Facebook	120,000,000,000	Rodriguez (2018)
2018	Facebook	16,000,000,000	Rodriguez (2018)
2018	Facebook	36,000,000,000	Rodriguez (2018)
2016	Samsung	96,700,000,000	Allen (2017)
2016	Mylan	4,300,000,000	Allen (2017)
2015	Valeant Pharmaceuticals	55,900,000,000	Allen (2017)
2015	Volkswagen	33,400,000,000	Allen (2017)
2015	Toshiba	7,800,000,000	Allen (2017)
2013	Lululemon	1,400,000,000	Allen (2017)
2013	Carnival Cruises	3,100,000,000	Allen (2017)
TOTAL		**609,400,000,000**	

2.8 Summary of Reputational Crisis Communication Research

The above literature is representative of the central theories and concepts in contemporary crisis communication research, which form the foundations of crisis communication literature and practice. Crisis communication research is focussed on determining the most effective communication strategy to reduce and limit the negative impact of a reputational crisis for an organisation or a person. The basic elements of crisis communication theory are complimentary to each other, and collectively can form a basis for practitioners dealing with reputational crises (see Fig. 2.1 below).

Unfortunately published crisis communication literature is lacking in diversity (Avery et al., 2010). Most reputational crisis communication research is concerned with stakeholder reactions to specific image restoration messages, and seeks to identify the most effective reputational crisis communication strategies for various

Fig. 2.1 Homogenised model of crisis communication strategies

crisis scenarious (Avery et al., 2010). Avery et al determined that crisis communication research would benefit from "more diverse contextual and methodological application" (2010, p. 190). Avery et al. (2010) echo Coombs' (1995) concerns that the context specific research would lead to a cumbersome volume of literature founded on a limited methodological application.

The context based crisis research means that the research findings are predominantly focussed on the effectiveness of situational crisis communication theory strategies and image restoration strategies. Audience responses to specific crisis communication strategies are the basis of extant literature. However, such research oftentimes fails to engage with how the crisis audience view the crisis itself. Instead most research adapts a company perspective of the crisis[3], or a theoretical assumption that categorises the offensive act of the crisis. From this point, research is typically focussed on which communication strategies are most effective, and does not engage with why those strategies are most effective. Instead of following such methodology, it may be more effective to determine specifically what stakeholders deem offensive about what the organisation is perceived to have done, and then address those concerns. For instance, Benoit (1995, 1997) provides a clear typology of which types of messages are more effective. Yet Benoit (1995, 1997) does not focus in on rationale to explain why certain types of messages are more effective, or what specific context or offensiveness these messages seek to address. In other words, identifying what the crisis' audience finds offensive and addressing that offensiveness may be more effective than developing a framework of the crisis based on the organisation's perspective. Jorgensen's (1996) method of applying

[3] This is likely in part due to the use of Freeman's (1984) stakeholder theory which places the company at the centre of all stakeholders.

Weiner's (1986) attribution theory is perhaps the most direct association between stakeholder responses and reputational crisis communication strategies, as Jorgensen (1996) provides insight into why stakeholders respond in a certain manner. A streamlined approach to reputational crisis communication strategies and messages should account for why certain messages are more effective (Lee, 2004) with stakeholders. This publication proposes to aid in understanding how different stakeholders view the offensive elements in crises. In a manner similar to Jorgensen (1996) applying attribution theory to explain stakeholder responses, this text aims to aid in understanding why stakeholders respond to reputational crises, as opposed to how stakeholders respond to certain messages.

2.9 Conclusion

Given the significance of Benoit and Coombs' contributions to the field, by measure of the large use of their research findings, this overview is brief. However the strategies they developed do not seem to be holistic, in that they are methods, as opposed to methodology. That is to say that they offer what is only a small part of dealing with reputational crises. Benoit's work, although detailed in his book (Benoit, 1995), only looked at the types of communication strategies available and which are most effective. Coombs (1995, 1998) only looked at what communication strategies are suitable for different crisis types.

Unfortunately, both Coombs and Benoit stopped short of deeply engaging what are arguably the important elements of any reputational crisis; that is the stakeholder. For without stakeholders, a crisis does not exist.

Possibly more problematic for crisis practitioners and academics following the research paths developed by Benoit and Coombs, is that neither of their approaches to dealing with crises, actually deal with crises. Instead they appear to seek a general size fits all solution in terms of communication, rather than trying to fix (a) why stakeholders are upset, and (b) how the crisis came about in the first place. Much is written in crisis lifecycle theory, which nearly always ends with a post mortem of a crisis. Though even the post mortem strategy generally fails to understand what why it went wrong from the stakeholder's perspective. Furthermore, dealing with the actual offensive act with a view to prevention and best practice, seems to be beyond the grasp of most existing crisis literature.

We should consider why and how stakeholders are offended by an action, and then address it from the stakeholder's perspective. The next chapter is dedicated the stakeholder theory to develop the idea that solving the concerns stakeholders have, is critical to ending a crisis and having a positive outcome for everyone. It is naïve to think that using a type of message is the most effective means to solving a crisis. When a crisis is solved just by a specific message type, it is more by luck than by comprehensive strategy, because the offensive act has not been completely dealt with and stakeholders been neither adequately considered nor satisfied. The causes of the crises often still remain, and the opportunity of growth through best practice have not yet been realised. Potentially more problematic, reputational crises will continue to occur as most western nations have laws that require corporate executives to place the company and its shareholders as a first priority. In the current dominant framework of reputational crises research, this means that reputational crises cannot easily be solved.

Bibliography

ABC News. (2013, October 10). *$40m class action launched against Cash Converters over short-term NSW loans*. Retrieved July 2020, from ABC News: https://www.abc.net.au/news/2013-10-10/2440m-class-action-launched-against-cash-coverters-over-loans/5014510

ABC. (2010a, December 21). *Dam there is no dam*. Retrieved July 2020, from ABC News: https://www.abc.net.au/news/2010-12-21/dam-there-is-no-dam/2381332

ABC. (2010b, April 29). *Rous Water denies fluoride environmental risk*. Retrieved July 2020, from ABC News: https://www.abc.net.au/news/2010-04-29/rous-water-denies-fluoride-environmental-risk/414424

Allen, K. (2017, August 28). *How much can a PR crisis cost you?* Retrieved August 17, 2019, from PR Daily: https://www.prdaily.com/how-much-can-a-pr-crisis-cost-you/

Alpanlan, C. M., Green, S. E., & Mitroff, I. (2009). Corporate governance in the context of crisis: Towards a stakeholder theory of crisis management. *Journal of Contingencies and Crisis Management, 17*(1), 38–49.

Anderson, A. G. (2014). Oil spills and crisis communication. In *Media, environment and the network society. Palgrave studies in media and environmental communication* (pp. 98–127). Palgrave Macmillan.

Australian Marine Conservation Society. (2015, December 10). *Australia's approval of Adani mine inconsistent with goals to protect and promote the Great Barrier Reef*. Retrieved December 2015, from Australian Marine Conservation Society: http://www.marineconservation.org.au/news.php/749/australias-approval-of-adani-mine-inconsistent-with-goals-to-protect-and-promote-the-great-barrier-r

Avery, E. J., Lariscy, R. W., Kim, S., & Hocke, T. (2010). A quantitative review of crisis communication research in public relations. *Public Relations Review, 36*(2), 190–192.

Benoit, W. L. (1995). *Accounts, excuses, and apologies: A theory of image restoration strategies*. Albany: State University of New York Press.

Benoit, W. L. (1997). Image repair discourse and crisis communication. *Public Relations Review*, 177–186.

Benoit, W. L., & Drew, S. (1997). Appropriatness and effectiveness of image repair strategies. *Communication Reports*, 153–163.

Black, E. (2012, Febuary 27). *IBM's Role in the Holocaust — What the New Documents Reveal*. Retrieved Febuary 2019, from Huffington Post: https://www.huffingtonpost.com/edwin-black/ibm-holocaust_b_1301691.html

Carmody, B. (2015, December 1). *Halal certification is a "purely commercial exchange" according to Senate inquiry*. Retrieved July 2020, from Smart Company: https://www.smartcompany.com.au/business-advice/politics/halal-certification-is-a-purely-commercial-exchange-according-to-senate-inquiry/

Commonwealth of Australia Senate. (2015, December 1). *Third party certification of food*. Retrieved July 2020, from Parliament of Australia: https://www.aph.gov.au/Parliamentary_Business/Committees/Senate/Economics/Food_Cert_Schemes/~/media/Committees/economics_ctte/Food_Cert_Schemes/report.pdf

Coombs, W. T. (1995). Choosing the right words: The development of guidelines for the selection of the appropriate crisis-response strategies. *Management Communication Quarterly, 8*, 447–476.
Coombs, W. T. (1998). An analytic framework for crisis situations: Better responses from a better understanding of the situation. *Journal of Public Relations Research, 10*(3), 177–191.
Coombs, W. T. (2007). *Ongoing crisis communication: Planning, managing and responding* (2nd ed.). Sage.
Coombs, W. T., Frandsen, F., Holladay, S. J., & Johansen, W. (2010). Why a concern for apologia and crosos communication. *Corporate Communications, 15*(4), 337–349.
Fink, S. (1986). *Crisis management: Planning for the inevitable*. Amacom.
Fodor, A., & Stowe, J. (2012). Financial market reactions to a company disaster: The BP case. *Journal of Applied Finance, 1*, 1–16.
Freeman, R. E. (1984). *Strategic management: A stakeholder approach*. Pitman Publishing Inc..
GetUp Australia. (2020). *About GetUp Australia*. Retrieved March 2020, from GetUp Australia: https://www.getup.org.au/about/
Greenhouse, S. (2009, October 30). *BP faces record fine for '05 refinery explosion*. Retrieved July 2020, from The New York Times: http://nytimes.com/2009/10/30/business/30labor.html
Griffin, L. M. (1952). The rhetoric of historical movements. *Quarterly Journal of Speech*, 184–188.
Heath, R. L. (1997). *Strategic issues management: Organisations and public policy challenges*. Sage.
Hermann, C. (1963). Some consequences of crisis which limit the viability of organisations. *Administrative Science Quarterly, 8*(1), 61–82.
Hern, A. (2020, July 1). *Third of advertisers may boycott Facebook in hate speech revolt*. Retrieved July 15, 2020, from The Guardian: https://www.theguardian.com/technology/2020/jun/30/third-of-advertisers-may-boycott-facebook-in-hate-speech-revolt
Hoff, J. (1984). *People in crisis: Understanding and helping*. Addison Wesley.
Hotten, R. (2015, December 10). *Volkswagen: The scandal explained*. Retrieved December 11, 2015, from BBC News: Business: http://www.bbc.com/news/business-34324772
Jaques, T. (2009). Learning from past crises: Do iconic cases help or hinder. *Public Relations Journal, 3*(1), 1–16.
Jorgensen, B. K. (1996). Components of consumer reaction to company-related mishaps: a structural equation model approach. *Advances in Consumer Research, 23*, 346–351.
Kim, S., Avery, E. J., & Lariscy, R. (2009). Are crisis communicators practising what we preach? An evaluation of crisis response strategy analyzed in public relations from 1991 to 2009. *Public relations Review, 35*, 446–448.
Lee, B. K. (2004). Audience-oriented approach to crisis communication: A study of Hong Kong consumers' evaluation of an organizational crisis. *Communication Research, 31*, 600–618.
Lerbinger, O. (1997). *The crisis manager: Facing risk and responsibility*. Lawrence Erblaum Associates Inc.
Lerbinger, O. (2006). *Corporate public affairs: Interacting with interest groups, media, and government*. Lawrence Erlbaum.
Lyall, S. (2010, July 12). *In BP's Record, a History of Boldness and Costly Blunders*. Retrieved July 2020, from The New York Times: https://www.nytimes.com/2010/07/13/business/energy-environment/13bprisk.html
McDonald, L. M., Sparks, B., & Glendon, A. I. (2010). Stakeholder reactions to company crisis communications and causes. *Public Relations Review, 36*, 262–271.
Mitroff, I. (1994). Crisis management and environmentalism: A natural fit. *California Management Review, 36*(2), 101–113.
Mitroff, I. (2005). *Why some companies emerge stronger and better from a crisis*. Amacom.
Mitroff, I., & Alpaslan, M. (2003). Preparing for evil. *Harvard Business Review, 81*, 109–115.
Nicolls, S. (2014, May 15). *Metgasco's Bentley gas drilling suspended, referred to ICAC*. Retrieved July 2020, from The Sydney Morning Herald: https://www.smh.com.au/national/nsw/metgascos-bentley-gas-drilling-suspended-referred-to-icac-20140515-zrd2w.html

Oxford Metrica. (2012). *Oxford Metrica Reputation Review*. Retrieved July 2020, from AON Risk Services: https://www.aon.com/attachments/risk-services/Aon-OM-Reputation-Review-2012.pdf

Pincus, T. H. (1985). A crisis parachute: Helping stock prices have a soft landing. *Journal of Business Strategy, 6*(4), 32–38.

Regester, M., & Larkin, J. (2008). *Risk issues and crisis management*. MPG Books Ltd..

Rodriguez, S. (2018, November 20). *Facebook's scandals in 2018 effect on stock*. Retrieved August 2019, from CNBC: https://www.cnbc.com/2018/11/20/facebooks-scandals-in-2018-effect-on-stock.html

Sabet, S., Cam, M., & Heaney, R. (2012). Sharemarket reaction to the BP oil spill and the US government moratorium on exploration. *Australian Journal of Management, 37*(1), 61–76.

Sakzewski, E. (2020, June 29). *A Facebook ad boycott has cost Mark Zuckerberg $72 billion. But will it make any difference?* Retrieved July 14, 2020, from ABC News: https://www.abc.net.au/news/2020-06-29/facebook-ad-boycott-costs-zuckerberg-7-billion-what-does-it-mean/12402062

Saunders, M. D. (2004). Patterns of conflict preceding a crisis: A case study analysis. In *Responding to crisis: A theoretical approach to crisis communication* (pp. 139–148). Lawrence Erlbaum Associates, Publishers.

SBS. (2015, November 5). *Muslim Australians regularly experience abuse and discrimination, report finds*. Retrieved July 2020, from SBS News: https://www.sbs.com.au/news/muslim-australians-regularly-experience-abuse-and-discrimination-report-finds

Schultz, W. (2004). Reconstructing mediatization as an analytical concept. *European Journal of Communication, 19*(1), 87–101.

Shrivastava, P., Mitroff, I., Miller, D., & Miglani, A. (1988). Understanding industrial crises. *Journal of management studies, 25*(4), 285–303.

Tench, R., & Jones, B. (2015). Social media: The Wild West of CSR communications. *Social Responsibility Journal, 11*(2), 290–305.

Ulmer, R., Sellnow, T., & Seeger, M. (2007). *Effective crisis communication*. Sage.

Ulmer, R., Sellnow, T., & Seeger, M. (2015). *Effective crisis communication: Moving from crisis to oppertunity*. Sage.

Vromen, A. (2008). Political change and the internet in Australia: Introducing GetUp. In T. Hayhtio & J. Rinne (Eds.), *Net working/networking: Citizen initiated internet politics* (pp. 103–126). Tampere University Press.

Weiner, B. (1986). *An attributional theory of motivation and emotion*. Springer.

Weisman, J., & Chazan, G. (2010, June 17). *BP Agrees to $20 Billion Fund*. Retrieved July 2020, from The Wall Street Journal: https://www.wsj.com/articles/SB10001424052748704198004575310571698602094

White, L. (2019, August 17). *Looking back on the legacy of Terania Creek*. Retrieved July 2020, from ABC News: https://www.abc.net.au/news/2019-08-17/looking-back-legacy-terania-creek/11420526?nw=0

Yin, R. K. (1993). *Applications of case study research*. Sage.

Chapter 3
Reputational Crisis Stakeholders – Fluidity in Identities

Abstract Critics of Freeman's early stakeholder theory suggested it is narcissistic in nature, but the popular simplified interpretation of stakeholder theory ensured that it is used by much vigour for anyone wishing to improve their own position. Hence it must have seemed like an easy means to establishing a crisis communication dialogue whereby the organisation at the centre of the crisis focuses on solving that crisis for its own benefit. Through understanding the roles these stakeholders play in reputational crises, it becomes clearer that a reputational crisis cannot exist without these stakeholders, and that the motivations of these stakeholders means that reputational crises will continue to occur.

Juxtaposing Freeman's more recent revisions of stakeholder theory with the advent of social media creates more complex stakeholder types. This also requires us to have a better understanding of stakeholder's viewpoints and motivations. A model to determine the salience of social media stakeholders in reputational crises is proposed to better understand how these actors can be influential and play an active role in developing a reputational crisis.

Remember the last time you did something really bad and it affected nobody and nobody knew about it? Maybe it happened, maybe it didn't? But without anyone knowing or being affected, nothing will come of it. But if you had people present or effected, it could well have turned into your own crisis. This is why stakeholders are arguably the most important element of any reputational crisis. This chapter looks at stakeholder theory, giving some background to how it evolved as it became more popular. The most common use of stakeholder theory is discussed against the backdrop of its popular contemporary inception. A basic overview of critique is discussed, including those of the founder of contemporary stakeholder theory. Next, the idea of salience of stakeholders is introduced and is used to understanding crisis stakeholders, their relevance, and importance. The nearly always present crisis stakeholder types are discussed in more detail and an overview of the varying stakeholders is provided. Stakeholder viewpoints and empathy as brought in as a means to be able to effectively

T. Schermer, *Reputational Crises Unspun*, https://doi.org/10.1007/978-981-16-5130-4_3

understand crisis stakeholders, and where necessary, discuss the stakeholders with their unique viewpoints in mind. Social media is reviewed in relation to how it has changed the crisis communications landscape for stakeholders, their roles and their influence.

The methodology of researching things often uses the categorisation of data into inflexible categories. Often the categorisations are contrived to suit the focus of research and situations. This challenge is also common to crisis communication, in academia and industry. Rigid frameworks and categorisations are an effective way to communicate, and to sort data to make sense of the masses of information and knowledge. Because of our ever increasing need for rapid information dissemination, the categorisation of everything will remain as the status quo. To research the phenomena of reputational crises, there are sometimes countless stakeholders, media releases, and messages. Therefore listing these in categories is still one of the most effective means to make sense of things, for us to be able analyse what we are looking for.

The categorisations discussed herein are only offered as concepts of this framework, and stakeholders may belong to more than one category or classification. Further complicating things; the level of stakeholder importance is always in a state of flux. For example, an interest group stakeholder can easily also become a media stakeholder, or be elected to government office, and become a politician as well as a member of an interest group. Stakeholder categorisations should remain fluid. As with this example, stakeholders can change and increase their influence through changing or increasing, and decreasing the influence in their position. However, the importance of stakeholders can also change as a result of the stakeholder's environment, and consequently their support base changing. For example, when animal rights activists stormed livestock farms (Rennie, 2019), the traditional news media quickly vilified their actions, calling them illegal. This swiftly resulted in the salience of those activists being affected. The activists' illegal trespassing activities made it more difficult for the group to gain or regain support from sympathetic politicians who need to reflect their constituent's values.

In summary, it is expedient to use categorisations and classifications. However, be wary that there is flux and fluidity in categorisations and classifications, and it is often difficult to perfectly use these to describe and understand any specific single stakeholder. Therefore a great amount of caution is advised in trying to find a "one size fits all approach" to crisis communication.

Despite these paradigm problems, we must contend with the current method of classification and categorisation, and as such discuss these in the context of those parameters. The next section offers stakeholder with descriptions to aid in understanding reputational crisis situation.

3.1 Without Stakeholders

"If a tree falls in the forest, and there is no one there to hear the crash, does it make a sound?". This common riddle suggests that when an event happens without anyone present, does it still exist? Or more philosophically, does it have even happen or have any relevance? In the same way, a reputational crisis without stakeholders is a non-event at the time that it happens. If for instance, a negative event occurs and no one who affected by it and no one holds the organisation to account, then the organisation's reputation is not affected. It is not a crisis. Simply put, a crisis without stakeholders is merely an event which is irrelevant, until it becomes relevant to a stakeholder, possibly at a later date. In many instances a seemingly non-threatening event in the past may be brought up by the media or stakeholder during a reputational crisis, and past event can be effective in demonstrating continued neglect or bad conduct.

This section first discusses the definition of stakeholder theory in terms of the commonly used concept authored by Freeman (1984). This is followed with a discussion of the revised stakeholder theory by Freeman et al. (2010). (In Chap. 5 the implications, problems, and solutions in the use of stakeholder theory in crisis communications are discussed). The next section discusses the salience of stakeholders in social media and how stakeholder dynamics and attributes have evolved as a result of media evolution. The remainder of this chapter looks at stakeholder types that are regulars in reputational crises, and the salience of crisis stakeholders. These descriptions serve as a preamble to media, setting out the background to resituating the stakeholder paradigm in reputational crises, the first steps to a more effective and cohesive strategy to solving reputational crises.

3.2 Stakeholder Theory

Stakeholders are of primary concern to reputational crisis communication, thus stakeholder theory is heavily relied upon in crisis communication (Alpaslan et al., 2009; Regester & Larkin, 2008). Crises not only impact organisations, they can also have a substantial impact on its stakeholders. Benoit (1997) noted that the effectiveness of a crisis communication message depends not only matching the crisis communications to the crisis characteristics, but also matching the crisis communications to the audience for the intended message. For instance, a communication for shareholders would be focussed on corporate profits and future growth, whereas a communication for customers would be more focussed on value for money, quality, and customer service. As such the application of stakeholder theory, is not just a means of identifying stakeholders, but also a means of categorising stakeholders, and is central to crisis communication strategies.

The objective of stakeholder theory is to allow an organisation to determine which parties matter to the organisation, and who should be taken into account in the organisation's planning and actions, so that the organisation can maximise it's potential in achieving it's primary objectives. This section discusses Freeman's (1984) stakeholder theory as the dominant stakeholder theory in communication (Mitchell et al., 1997), providing the background to the resulting issues in the theory and practice of reputational crisis communication. First an overview of Freeman's (1984) stakeholder theory and model is discussed, followed by a review of the Freeman et al. (2010) revised stakeholder model and concluded with a review of a stakeholder salience model.

3.2.1 Freeman's Stakeholder Theory

Freeman's *Strategic Management: A stakeholder approach* (1984) provides the framework for the contemporary theory and model of stakeholder identification employed today in organisations and in reputational crisis communication. Freeman's theory and his diagram, "a stakeholder view of the firm" (Freeman, 1984), provide a means to identify of stakeholder groups, and determine their relevance to corporations (Mitchell et al., 1997; Frow & Payne, 2011; Key, 1999). The diagram placed in the first chapter of the book likely became a focal point for those seeking to skip reading the entire book and instead take in the diagram as a snapshot of the complete theory. In the diagram, the "firm" was situated at the centre, and surrounded by all stakeholders. The stakeholders are connected by double ended arrows to the firm, to illustrate the to-and-fro between the firm and the stakeholders. In this, the stakeholders listed are; governments, local community organisations, owners, consumer advocates, customers, competitors, media, employees, special interest groups, environmentalists, and suppliers (Freeman, 1984, p. 6).

While working as a researcher at university, Freeman developed the theory after being requested to provide a model for companies to determine who they should deal with to increase corporate efficiencies (Freeman et al., 2004). The founding principle for stakeholder theory originated from a request to Freeman to create a "window to the world" (Freeman, 2004, p. 228). Freeman established that;

> a party is a stakeholder is if the party can affect the organisation, or can be affected by the organisation (Freeman, 1984)

Freeman's stakeholder model was rapidly adopted by business, government, and academia, as evidenced by the prolific use of the term today. The principles of this stakeholder theory were designed to focus specifically on corporations, as illustrated in Freeman's (1984) model.

As most theories that become popular and are adopted into mainstream use, stakeholder theory drew a variety of reviews. Key (1999) examplified the divide between stakeholder theory and shareholder theory, suggesting stakeholder theory is "essentially a narcissistic theory. That is, it places the organisation in the realm of the child in terms of development. It is at the centre of its universe, and while it is connected to others, its main role is to ensure that these others serve its needs with a minimum conflict" (Key, 1999, p. 324). Key (1999) pointed out that the stakeholder model positioned the organisation as central and hence pivotal to the stakeholders. Key's argument suggests in this model, stakeholders are only considered as a means to serve the organisation's end goals, rather than a symbiotic relationship between organisation and stakeholder.[1] Key's (1999) arguments are quite divisive. However it does seem that Freeman succeeded in developing a concept that allowed a company to view its stakeholders through a window to the world, as the central placement of the firm in relation to stakeholders in Freeman's (1984) stakeholder theory does indeed appear like a window to the world. Despite Key's (1999) criticism of Freeman's (1984) corporate centric stakeholder theory, Freeman later noted (2004, p. 229) "When the main academic audience for my ideas became people who taught business and society or corporate social responsibility or business ethics I was surprised". Freeman's (1984) first stakeholder model clearly identifies environmentalists, employees, local community organisations and consumer advocates. These stakeholders are identified as primary concerns in corporate social responsibility (Freeman et al., 2010; International Organisation for Standardization, 2011), which suggests that Freeman's (1984) stakeholder theory, though company centric, has led to more stakeholder focussed corporate strategies being developed.

Although Freeman's (1984) stakeholder theory was extensive, the actual publication is rarely read in its entirety (Freeman et al., 2010). This led to the common use of an over-simplified interpretation of the (1984) stakeholder theory (Freeman et al., 2010), which may have contributed to the popularisation of the stakeholder model. Following two decades of further developing stakeholder theory, Freeman wrote *the stakeholder approach revisited* (2004), seeking to correct misconceptions about his 1984 publication. In this Freeman stated "We defined 'stakeholder' in a broad strategic sense as 'any group or individual that can affect or is affected by the achievement of a corporation's purpose" (Freeman, 2004, p. 229). Freeman et al. later sought to redress the corporate organisation bias perceived as an element of his original stakeholder theory, with the publication of *Stakeholder theory: The state of the art* (Freeman et al., 2010), offering a revised stakeholder model.

Freeman et al. (2010) retained the corporation's place at the centre of the model. Althought the corporation is central to the revised model, the essence of the revision is nearly solely focussed on the stakeholders. The revised stakeholder model employs a more inclusive concept with various stakeholders and stratifies stakeholders as primary or secondary stakeholders. In this, the communities, customers, financiars, suppliers, and employees are regarded as primary stakeholders, and government, media, special interest groups, and consumer advocate groups, are listed as secondary stakeholders.

The new stakeholder model is more descriptive of the various elements present in the common corporate environment. For instance, Freeman's (1984) initial model

[1] Freeman, as the progenitor of stakeholder theory, took issue with the stakeholder model usage and specifically the notion that stakeholders only exist to serve the organisation in attaining its end goals (Freeman, 2004).

did not include financiars or communities,[2] which are often important crisis stakeholders (Lerbinger, 1997). As such, the new model is more suitable to be employed in reputational crisis research to identify more crisis stakeholders.

3.2.2 *Stakeholder Theory Problems in Crisis Communication*

"Having one objective function makes governance and management difficult. It is hard to imagine how anyone can look at the recent wave of business scandals, all of which are orientated toward ever increasing shareholder value at the expense of other stakeholders, and argue that this philosophy is a good idea" (Freeman et al., 2004, p. 366).

In terms of reputational crisis management, this statement suggests that the application of stakeholder theory should perhaps include a less organisation centric perspective and instead consider the organisation from the stakeholder's perspective. The principle of having the company at the centre as the most important element in that model does not reflect the primary objective of crisis communications. That is to say; although crisis communicators act to achieve the objective of the company, they can only do so by focussing on what is considered offensive from the stakeholder's perspective, and thus the crisis should be the main focus point and at the centre of all stakeholders.

3.3 Stakeholder Empathy

Unfortunately as reputational crises are by nature time critical, it is often the case that stakeholder perspectives are only considered very hurriedly thus often in a very basic and superficial manner. However as reputational crises do not exist without the presence of stakeholders it is important to try to develop the stakeholder perspective more thoroughly. Coming from the idea that most stakeholders view things from their own unique perspective, and that all stakeholders can be important, it is imperative to attempt to understand reputational crises from the unique stakeholder perspectives. In other words; empathy. The main obstacles to consider in this stakeholder empathy are;

(a) People in seemingly similar situations may have varying viewpoints,
(b) People in similar situations may have varying viewpoints.

[2]Freeman did include 'local community organisations'. Referring to them as organisations, suggests that they are an organised group with specific shared objectives. For the purpose of this chapter, the notion of communities means individuals who do not act as a collective or organisation, and the foremost common attribute that these individuals share in terms of stakeholders, is that they reside or operate in a shared area.

To understand this better we must first seek to understand what influences those stakeholder perspectives. Prima facie, it is easy to understand a stakeholder's perspective because we can only apply what we know of our stakeholders to develop an empathetic viewpoint. However as we have learned growing through life, everyone has different experiences, and those previous experiences develop our viewpoints on contemporary situations. For example, a Florida fisherman whose business was affected by the BP oil spill would be extremely upset with the proposal of another deep sea oil rig being installed, whereas a fisherman, who was not affected by the BP Gulf of Mexico oil spill, is far less likely to be concerned with a proposal of a deep sea oil rig. Though both are fisherman and are operating in an area that could be impacted by a new deep sea oil rig, they have different viewpoints based on their experiences through life. This example shows how two seemingly similar stakeholders can have different viewpoints based on their experiences.

This is further complicated with the notion that although two people can share the same event, in the same way, yet their viewpoints are uniquely different. A personal example of this would be a couple in a domestic relationship. Through most of their lives, a wife and husband share the same situations as in they eat the same meals, face the same financial stresses, live in the same dwelling and sleep in the same bed. Thus seemingly they have the same experiences. However, their experiences of any singular event could be vastly different. Though their viewpoints are in part developed through their values (which would most likely be very similar as they are a couple), these viewpoints are also informed through their previous life experiences. Even though the couple share the same economic situation, they have different ideas about how to improve matters. One partner might find it more important to repaint the exterior of their house whilst the other demands that the inside of the house is more important and should be painted first. The arguments could be that the newly painted house will have more street appeal and thus increase the value of their house, whilst the other partner insists that painting the inside of the house will have a significant impact on their psyches and thus improve their happiness and possibly even their confidence leading to a promotion and pay increase at work which would also increase their economic prospects. In other words, although both have the same end goal of improving their economic situation, they have competing methods for achieving that ambition. A comparable corporate situation could involve one executive pushing for budget cuts to improve the bottom line, whereas another might focus on increasing sales focus to more profitable ventures, also increasing the bottom line.

These examples serve to explain that although some stakeholders might have had exactly the same experiences as a result of the crisis, their viewpoints on how a crisis should be solved, or the offending act that caused the crisis, be made good by way of compensation or environmental rehabilitation, they may have very different viewpoints on how to achieve this. And although it is impossible to walk in another's shoes and have their own lifetime of experiences that inform decisions, attitudes, and thoughts, it is important to at least seek to understand their primary concerns in relation to the offending act that led to the crisis.

3.4 Finding the Stakeholders

The use of stakeholder theory in crisis communications comes with some obstacles. For instance, if a stakeholder is an entity that can be affected by the company, or affect the company, then it is a prerequisite that the entity can be identified. Lerbinger asserts "stakeholders who are actual or potential participants in dealing with the issue must be listed and analysed" (1997, p. 323). However prior to a crisis it is difficult to identify every entity that could be affected by an unpredictable event. As the crisis progresses through the lifecycle and crisis impacts are becoming obvious more stakeholders may become visible (Lerbinger, 1997). For example, during the BP Deepwater Horizon oil spil claimants for damages as a result of the spill included fisherman and real estate agents who lost income as a result of the spill affecting the ecological environment (BP Claims, 2015; Staff and wire reports, 2010). In typical day to day operations, BP would not be able to foresee that fisherman and real estate agents would have any connection with the company, and thus it would be nearly impossible to identify these as stakeholders. Furthermore, during the first stages of the crisis these stakeholders as compensation claimants are not identifiable in Freeman's (1984) model, and perhaps only in the subsequent model by Freeman et al. (2010) as secondary or tertiary stakeholders.

3.5 Stakeholder Conflicts and Allegiances in Reputational Crises

Applying stakeholder theory only in the elementary function, that is, simply identifying stakeholders in crisis communications, neglects to consider the relevance of relationships between stakeholders. The relationships between various stakeholders may also impact a company during a reputational crisis (Lerbinger, 1997). For example, the anti-Halal certification action groups took actions against the retailers of Halal certified foods. Islam 4 Infidels suggested to their supporters that they purchase Halal certified cadbury chocolate from Woolworths supermarkets, open the packet outside the store, and then return it for a full refund (Islam4infidels, 2014). Thus from the perspective of Cadbury, the supermarket is their customer, the supermarket customers are Cadbury's end product consumers, of whom some are part of an anti-Halal interest group, who are by their affiliation in conflict with Cadbury the supernarket.

The relationships amongst stakeholders in reputational crises are not always based on conflict. Crises can bring stakeholder groups together with shared interests. For instance, environmental lobbyists may develop an allegiance with a government's natural resources division to pursue a moritorium on mining. Similarly, the coal seam gas industry in Australia found a stronger than expected opposition in what seemd an unlikely allegiance of some stakeholders. Two stakeholder groups that were previously opposed in the usage of land, farmers and conservationists, formed the Lock The Gate Alliance to jointly fight the coal seam gas industry's attempts to exploit farming land and natural habitats for mining (Jaques & Galloway, 2012).

Finally, companies that are under normal circumstances competitors, may during a reputational crisis form a temporary allegiance to protect their industry from increases in legislation, such as during the government imposed moratorium which temporarily banned deep sea oil platforms in the Gulf of Mexico, following the BP Deepwater Horizon oil spill (Fodor & Stowe, 2012). In that instance, it was in the interest of oil companies working in the Gulf of Mexico to work together towards having the moritarorium lifted. Hence the relationships between stakeholders can be important in crisis communications, in terms of how the allegiances are formed, and how these impact the organisation.

3.6 Stakeholder Theory in Traditional and Social Media

When Freeman developed stakeholder theory in 1984, the principles for identifying a stakeholder meant that the media could be identified as a stakeholder to companies (Freeman, 1984). By this definition, in the modern social media environment any person or group can act as a media outlet, and following Freeman's (1984) theory, these can thus be identified similar as a media outlet. Hence the methods and systems for dealing with the original version of media are no longer suitable (Coombs & Holladay, 2014). For instance, in the 1980's the news media (in its Fourth Estate role) could generally be relied upon to have certain commitments towards accountability, and to a large degree quality news media organisations could be relied upon to employ certain standards. Although for news media organisations acting in the social media environment the traditional expectations of accountability and standards are still applied, the same standards cannot be expected of all social media participants.

In the traditional news media environment corporations often enjoyed the benefits of disproportionate economic and other resources to ensure it has greater influence in communication channels (Bruce & Soloman, 2013), including the corporation's ability to communicate during reputational crises. The corporation's wealth was significantly larger than that of a consumer, thus a corporation could ensure it had proportionately larger media presence through the purchase of advertising space and influence. However in social media a consumer can gain as much attention as a large corporation. What was once a large disparity between the media presence of a company and that of a consumer has significantly reduced and the stakeholder relationship attributes should have changed accordingly.

3.6.1 Stakeholder Theory Complications in Social Media

Popular stakeholder theory was developed approximately 30 years before the advent of social media, and as such the original model did not take into account the proliferation of (social) media producers, and many existing stakeholders also becoming media producers (albeit often in the most amateur manner). Consequently stakeholder theory based corporate governance models did not allow for dealing with the social media situation, and led to hastened and sometimes panic driven attempts by corporations to develop a social media presence (Schermer & McKenna, 2015). Often due to the accelerated and hastily construed ideas many corporations were not capable of dealing with so many stakeholders, stakeholder complexities (Bruce & Soloman, 2013), and inter-relationships (Coombs & Holladay, 2014).

In the pre-social media era during which stakeholder theory and crisis communication strategies were developed, the overlap between end product consumers and media producers was nominal (Fig. 3.1). Nearly all end product consumers were also media consumers, but there were very few media producers.

Due to social media, any person can now qualify as a stakeholder as an end-product consumer, media consumer, and media producer (see Fig. 3.2).

These many multiple stakeholder role overlaps due to social media means that organisations often have to respond to many consumer's social media comments and publications. This becomes very complicated and is often impossible to resource sufficiently. Typically now, if a consumer is unhappy with a product or service, they are likely to post on the company's social media, airing their complaints for all other current and future customers to see. Many companies struggle with this as the volume of social media responses can grow exponentially and elicit more than a thousand complaints per hour. Complicating the issue further is that (a) most companies do not train their social media staff in crisis communication,

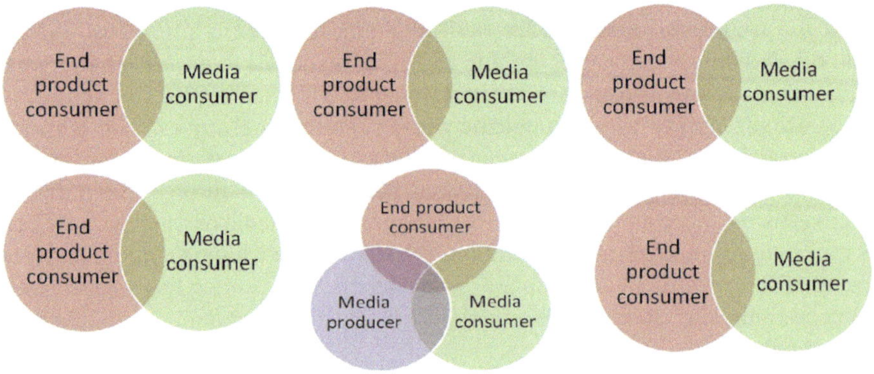

Fig. 3.1 Basic crisis stakeholder map prior to social media

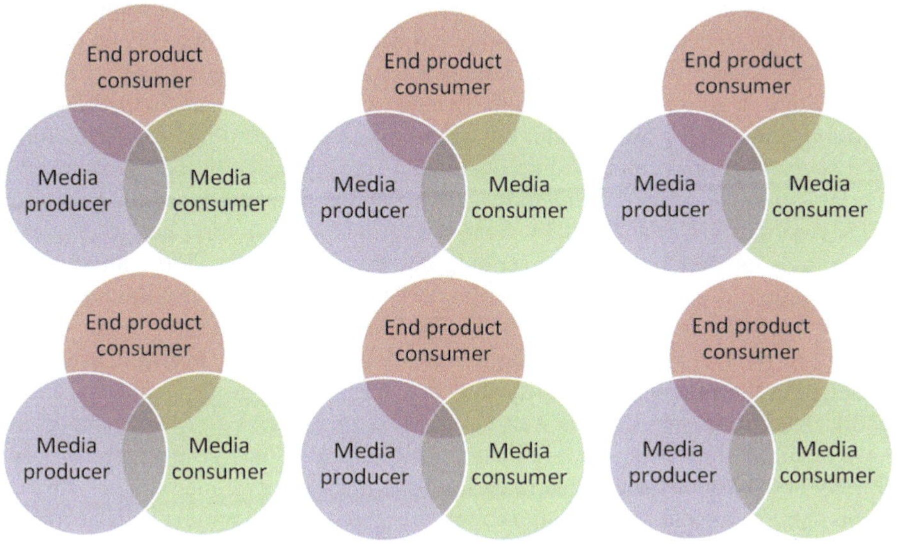

Fig. 3.2 Basic crisis stakeholder map since social media

and this a situation can quickly become out of control, and (b) many organisations outsource their social media content, which leaves the organisation out of touch with their audience which could lead to an instant public outrage in social media, where the organisation is held to account for statement it didn't make and possibly doesn't know the intent behind the statement, and is thus unable to address the concerns.

3.6.2 Accountability and Representation in Traditional and Dynamic Social Media

Applying the popular basic concept of stakeholder theory in crisis communication is not congruent with the hybrid nature of social media. Because social media is by nature founded in the public domain, each entity, be it a large company or single person, is represented individually and with equal voice as any other entity (Bruce & Soloman, 2013). This contrasts with the traditional disparity in how individuals and larger companies and organisations are represented in traditional society and media. For instance, the physical presence of a large corporation in traditional media is often congruent with the economic power of that organisation. In the social media environment, each participant, be it a large corporation or individual person, appears to have the same authority, rights and limitations (Bruce & Soloman, 2013). Despite this, often the corporate social responsibility and corporate governance methods employed in the traditional news media are directly employed in social media without updating those corporate social responsibility and corporate governance systems and methods to reflect the new environment (Sora et al., 2014). Although those corporate governance methods for engaging and valuing stakeholder contributions in the traditional platforms have been successful, they appear to be unsuitable for dealing with the dynamic, fast moving, and sometimes anonymous environment of social media (Johnston, 2015; Coombs & Holladay, 2014; Sora et al., 2014). The hybrid nature of social media, as a tool for information sending and receiving with a large numbers of participants, places it outside the parameters of traditional information distribution services (Bruce & Soloman, 2013). This unique aspect of information distribution not only challenges the traditional information news media distribution models, but also the accountability that was relied upon in the traditional news media. Traditional news media was, and still is, accountable to the owners of the news media organisation, news industry ethics associations, government legislation, and civil actions such as defamation. In contrast, social media users are not accountable to anyone, and through anonymity, such as fake social media accounts (Tench & Jones, 2015), can more easily avoid defamation claims. The social media model places information dissemination into the hands of anyone without any requirement of accuracy, media ethics, or accountability (Bruce & Soloman, 2013). Hence social media can and does carry with it a greater risk of spreading unreliable and incorrect information. Examples of unreliable social media ranges from the hacked AFP twitter account stating the White House was attacked (Moore & Roberts, 2013), to claims of riots in a London burger restaurant (Proctor et al., 2011). The implications that follow from such lack of accountability and responsibility, combined with the potential of an individual or small interest group effectively developing a greater social media audience than a corporation, shows the traditional methodology of stakeholder engagement as an outdated and ineffective model. Further compounding stakeholder management issues, throughout the last decade many collective interest groups have formed on social media, with some of these groups achieving significant success in furthering the development of their respective causes (GetUp Australia, 2020; Shirky, 2011). Such successes inspired a proliferation of social media action groups seeking to influence social, economic and political agendas in corporations and governments alike (Shirky, 2011).

These implications for stakeholder theory as employed in social media for corporate social responsibility and corporate governance, suggest that the existing models are no longer fitting. Mitchell et al. (1997) proposed a model of stakeholder management whereby stakeholder salience could be catagorised on the basis of urgency, legitimacy and power. Their model, when applied in a rudimentary form, aids in illustrating the significant differences between social media activist groups when the prima facie attributes of the social media groups appear similar (Schermer & McKenna, 2015).

More recent studies have focussed only on the legitmacy of stakeholders as a means improve stakeholder management (Tihanyi et al., 2014; Schermer & McKenna, 2015). With the view of improving corporate governance in reputational crises, Schermer & McKenna (2015) extrapolated the stakeholder salience model by Mitchell et al. (1997). Taking the Mitchell et al.'s (1997) three criteria of power, urgency, and legitimacy, Schermer and McKenna (2015) removed 'power' and 'urgency' as power is more fluid in reputational crises, and urgency is inherent in reputational crises. The legitimacy criterion by Mitchell et al. (1997) provided a platform for use in social media, where the increase in activity is rapidly becoming an important aspect of reputational crises. Schermer and McKenna (2015) seperated legitimacy into five sub-criteria, namely;

1. "Legitimacy of impact on stakeholder – are the stakeholders personally affected by the issue
2. "Political legitimacy – do the stakeholders have political affiliations which can in turn lead to policy influence?
3. "Corporate legitimacy – do the stakeholders engage with the business, or are they opposed to negotiation or discussion?
4. "Physical legitimacy – do the stakeholders have a physical presence?
5. "Societal legitimacy – do the stakeholders behave in a manner congruent to socially acceptable conduct? Do the stakeholders appeal to mainstream society, and thereby increase support for their cause?" (Schermer & McKenna, 2015, p. 8)

It is not uncommon now for reputational crises to attract thousands of social media participants to comment on an organisation's actions. These criteria can be helpful when attempting to determine who is a salient social media stakeholder. It can also be useful in understanding if these stakeholders have the ability to influence the organisation, or be influenced by the organisation, beyond the realms of the social media landscape.

List of Crisis Stakeholders

The following list of crisis stakeholders (Table 3.1) is generalised, simply because it is presumptive to use specific classifications as those will never adequately describe all stakeholder types, groups, affiliations, alliances, sub-groups, and so forth.

(It is important to remember that many of these entities can be stakeholders in numerous ways. For example a media consumer could be an end product consumer as well as a shareholder and a politician representing a government department).

Table 3.1 Stakeholders common to reputational crises

Crisis specific stakeholders	Organisation orientated stakeholders	Group orientated stakeholders	Public
Injured/aggrieved persons	Employees	Employee union	Emergency services
Families of the affected	Customers	Social media contributors	Industry regulators
Witnesses	Consumers	Social media consumers	Publics (not offended)
Crisis manager/consultant	Third party reseller	Special interest groups	Insurance companies
Crisis insurance company	Suppliers	Interest groups	Politicians – incumbent – Local
Offended publics	Management	Traditional news media – reporters	Politicians – incumbent – State
Claimants – current	Share holders	Traditional news media – institution	Politicians – incumbent – Federal
Claimants – (not yet visible)	Stock exchange regulators	Traditional news media consumers	Politician's staff
	Financier/banks	Interest groups legal representations	Local Government departments
	Investment brokers	Competitors	State Government departments
	Board of directors	Industry associations	Federal Government departments
	Organisation's media liaison	Consumer advocacy groups	Public prosecutors
	Organisation's legal counsel		Political lobbyists
	CEO, COO, CFO		Politician – Candidates
	Ethical governance panel/s		
	Organisation's insurance companies		
	Operations manager		
	Communications manager		

3.7 Who Is Important in a Crisis

Following Freeman's (1984) stakeholder theory and its popular adaptations, Mitchell et al. (1997) realised the importance of developing a model for determining stakeholder salience. Amongst the many adaptations and extensions of Freeman's (1984) stakeholder theory, the Mitchel et al. (1997) contribution is possibly the most useful (Neville et al., 2011).

As discussed earlier, the popular adaptation of Freeman's (1984) original theory meant that anyone who can be affected by an organisation, or can affected an organisation is a stakeholder. In most environments this means a nearly incomprehensible number of stakeholders which, due to sheer numbers, are difficult to categorise. For instance if we look at a local supermarket to identify its stakeholders; each single one of the suppliers, staff, customers, individuals who live/work/visit the environment in which it operates is a stakeholder. That amounts to a massive number of people to take into account. This brief example doesn't take into account the massive corporate structures, government agencies, and numerous other third parties with whom the supermarket has some sort of stakeholder relationship. Then when trying to map stakeholders, or allocate resources to managing aspects of stakeholder relationships (with the supermarket it could be workplace health and safety for example), the number of stakeholders make this task insurmountable.

Particularly in reputational crises when time is pressurized, it can be critical to determine who the important stakeholders are. "The inaccurate assessment of stakeholder claims has the potential to cause the organisation considerable financial and reputational harm" (Neville et al., 2011, p. 357).

For example if you are drafting a crisis communication message to be sent to stakeholders, a general stakeholder map may include one million television news viewers of whom most live and work outside the affected area and who other than that might only be stakeholders who are end product consumers. In other words, many receivers of crisis communication messages might not be effected stakeholders at all. Significant caution must be exercised to ensure that unaffected (non-crisis) stakeholders are not likely to be drawn into crisis conflicts unnecessarily.

Similarly, it wouldn't serve well to draft a crisis communication message to only a very small number of stakeholders. It is very useful to be able to determine which stakeholders matter, how they matter, when they matter, and why they matter.

Mitchell et al. wrote *Toward a theory of stakeholder identification and salience* (1997) with the intent of helping determine which stakeholders matter, and in terms of crisis communication when time is pressurized, this is most usefull. Their idea was about "the degree to which managers give priority to competing stakeholder claims" (Mitchell et al., 1997, p. 854) The authors proposed that a stakeholder's salience can be determined using three different criteria. These being:

(a) Power – how much power a stakeholder has to influence outcomes to their own preference, against the power of others to bring about an alternate outcome (Mitchell et al., 1997).
(b) Legitimacy – the authors use legitimacy as "a desirable social good, that it is something larger and more shared than a mere self-perception, and that it may be defnied and negotiated differently at various levels of social organization" (Mitchell et al., 1997, p. 867).
(c) Urgency – This is based on the two attributes of (a) time-sensitivity (which is central to crisis communication theories) and the (b) critically, as it related to the critical nature of the stakeholder's "claims call for immediate attention" (Mitchell et al., 1997, p. 867).

Stakeholder Power

The notion of a stakeholder's power in a reputational crisis is arguably fluid in a reputational crisis, as at the commencement of a crisis a stakeholder might be severly impacted by the crisis event, and because the crisis has just happened, the stakeholder has not yet realised their power to influence their outcomes. An example of this may be a stakeholder who has lost their home due to the crisis event and at the initial stage, feels powerless to pursue the large corporation that caused them to lose their home. However as the crisis progresses, the stakeholder may engage with lawyers, a politician, a government arbitrator, interest groups, and the news media. These actions would empower the stakeholder with sufficient social, political, and legal power to seek compensation for their losses.

Stakeholder Legitimacy

The precondition of legitimacy has siginificant importance during a crisis, as it can relate to the salience of the stakeholder's claim, be it ethical or a claim of compensation. For instance, a stakeholder might be a stakeholder by the reasoning that she is affected through being offended by the organisation's crisis causing act. However if that stakeholder is affected directly by the crisis through personal or financial loses as a direct result of the crisis, then the stakeholder has a more significant claim with the organisation, both by the stakeholder's own perception and society's perceptions.

Stakeholder Urgency

Unlike the power and legitimacy constructs of a stakeholder's claim, the urgency of a stakeholder's claim in a crisis is less susceptable to change and thus often more stable. Due to the time pressurized environment of a crisis, many things that happen and many stakeholders can be considered urgent. In most crisis situations, a stakeholder's claim is either urgent or it is not.

Mitchell et al. (1997) propose that the combination of all three elements; power, legitmacy, and urgency, provide a more accurate tool for determing a stakeholder's salience. However, Mitchell et al. pre-condition this with the notion that a stakeholder's salience is in a state of flux and can change. This state of flux is due to "1. Stakeholder attributes are variable, not steady state. 2. Stakeholder attributes are socially constructed, not objective, reality. 3. Consciousness and willful exercise may or not be present" (Mitchell et al., 1997, p. 868).

Primarily the first point that stakeholders salience is in a state of flux, because their attributes are in a state of flux, has significant relevance in a crisis. It means that a current stakeholder's crisis based situation can change from significantly affected to not at all affected, and as more common in the first stages of a crisis, a non-affected stakeholder can change into being an affected stakeholder, and thereby increase their salience during a crisis.

Using the ideas posited by Mitchell et al. (1997) we can make some more progress towards understand how social media stakeholders have risen to prominence in terms of salience. The graph below (Fig. 3.3) illustrates how social media plays a role in stakeholder salience.

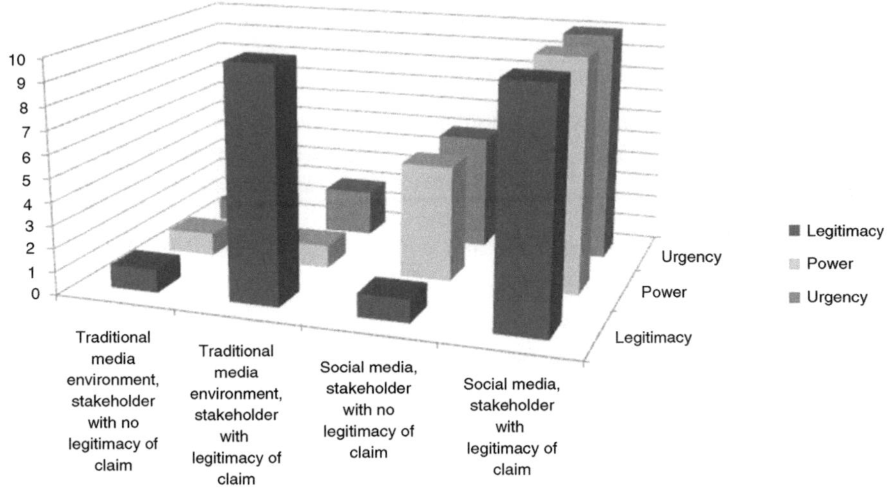

Fig. 3.3 Social media stakeholder salience in reputational crises

By the virtue of legitimacy, the social media stakeholder quickly becomes a legitimate stakeholder.

In the first example the stakeholder has no legitimacy of claim against a company and was restricted by the high costs of advertising his claim in the traditional media. This effectively means a crisis without more than one stakeholder. In the second example the stakeholder does have a legitimate claim, but again not the financial means to publicise the claim against the company to bring about a crisis. The third example has become a common feature in contemporary social media whereby a stakeholder does have the ability to develop their own media campaign through social media, but without a legitimate claim, the stakeholder will nearly always struggle to be salient. In the fourth example, the stakeholder with a legitimate claim can through social media effectively petition the company, legislators, company suppliers, exisiting customers, politicians, and potential customers, to name a few, to seek the company to address the stakeholders claim. The sheer extent of social media reach to other stakeholders can quickly escalate a badly handled salient stakeholder claim into a reputational crisis.

Salient Crisis Stakeholders

The stakeholder salience frame work offered by Mitchell et al. (1997) can be very useful during a reputational crisis. The state of flux of stakeholders does however complicate things again to some degree. Although every reputational crisis is unique, there often are stakeholder types present that are nearly always salient. These being:

- Directly affected stakeholders
- Encumbent politicians
- News media

- Legistlated authority
- Interest groups
- Organisation (experiencing the crisis)

These commonly recurring stakeholder types are nearly always by their nature salient stakeholders. The next section discusses the attributes of these stakeholders, in as much as possible generic terms with the view to include all those types stakeholders in stakeholder identification purposes. Though often they are all salient by nature, the salience of these groups, and within these groups, does differ during different times in a reputational crisis.

Directly Affected Stakeholders

It is the common to think of the organisation as 'the one experiencing the crisis'. This is the accepted terminology and it follows how crisis communication literature describes a crisis and the organisation. Unfortunately it is symptomatic of the issue in the common use of stakeholder theory and consequently crisis communication theory, in that it doesn't account for directly affected stakeholders as the potential central stakeholder.

The directly affected stakeholders are unique to each crisis. Often these stakeholders are the immediate victims of the crisis event. Be it they have been injured, lost their lives, lost their savings, or are suffering in some other way. These stakeholders are often the most emotionally charged and are not scared of voicing their outrage about their losses and demanding better industry practices.

Due to the unique nature of these stakeholders, it would be presumptive to list all their descriptions as they differ significantly with each different crisis. Despite this, it is critical to understand how these stakeholders have been adversely affected, and to seek to develop a genuine empathy and understanding with the objective of solving the crisis.

<u>Incumbent politicians</u> – These 'sitting politicians' are often vocal when something goes wrong and they can't be blamed for it. At the risk of generalising, incumbent politicians often embrace the opportunity to jump in front of the news camera and proclaim their disgust with the organisation that is accused of wrongdoing. Most often in doing so, they will take the moral high ground and occasionally demand for better industry practices.

<u>News media (reporters)</u> – These stakeholders can be large in numbers, but often only a few are leading the news media industry, and by that virtue they are empowered to frame the crisis as they see it. This group of stakeholders can be seen from their organisational obligations (in that they have obligations to their employers to produce leading news), and from their journalistic integrity obligation (where they have to maintain standards not just for what they produce, but how they produce it). Thus their motivations are often conflicted between producing a story that will lead the day's news media, and their ethically based motivations for producing an honest news story.

<u>Legislated authority</u> – Strictly speaking this category includes emergency response workers, but in the greater context of the crisis and explaining their role in solving the reputational crises, the legislated authority is the government

mandated (thus legal) overseer of actions which include the offending act which started the crisis, and has a significant role in drafting policy proposals for politicians to take to their government to vote on, turning them into law. For example, in a crisis pertaining to the management of superannuation funds, the legislated authority is one that oversees such activities (i.e. an investment commission). In a consumer food crisis in America, the Food and Drug Administration is the legislated authority that has oversight and the legal authority to shut down distribution of an organisation's product. These legislated authorities can have a significant impact on how an industry goes about its business, and can at times shut down entire divisions of business operations for many companies. For example the moratorium on deep sea drilling, that was enacted by the US government during the BP Deepwater Horizon crisis.

Interest groups – An interest group is a collective of individuals who share a common social goal or environmental interest and pursue a change in public policy or corporate agendas to protect that common interest.

In the day to day operations an organisation may be aware of interest groups that seek to influence their operations or the public policy of their operations, but may not feel the need to engage with them as they do not pose a significant threat to the business practices.

Whilst an organisation may be trying to deal with the impacts and fall out of a reputational crisis, interest groups will often be tempted to inflame the crisis further to gain ground on their objectives. The crisis caused media attention will be embraced by both politicians and the interest groups.

Related interest groups will embrace the opportunity to engage with the news media to state that their concerns were well founded, and oftentimes call on relevant politicians to push through policy changes to ensure the act which caused the reputational crisis won't happen again.

Naturally not all interest groups will engage in the reputational crisis, unless it is relevant to them. The closer the crisis causing act or crisis impact is to the nature of their objective as an interest group, the more they will engage with the crisis, including other stakeholder such as the media, politicians, legislators, and afflicted and/or aggrieved stakeholders.

Oftentimes an interest group will not reduce their engagement with the crisis until (a) the crisis is over and no longer has the media attention, or (b) the situation of the crisis has through stakeholders or the interest group themselves, brought about the change that the interest group was seeking.

A combination of things will often lead to the interest group's membership increase as a direct result of the crisis. Namely;

(a) The media attention on the issue created by the crisis will increase membership as individuals become aware of the group's general ambitions
(b) Members of the public will join the interest group to stop future offending acts such as the one that led to the crisis

(c) The politicisation and mediation of the crisis will attract some new members to align themselves with popular group activities.[3]

Not often, though sometimes interest groups can have significant financial resources to further their cause, and oftentimes they already have existing relationships with incumbent politicians.

Interest groups are most often organised into structures and some have extensive hierarchies within the group. Some interest groups have become more precise in their methodology, using lobbying methods, mass online activity, choreographed protests, and professionally developed media content and engagement. An established interest group is often equipped with slogans and key messages, and if the crisis is closely related to their cause, they will have a significant impact on how the offensive action that led to the crisis is framed.

It is important to not alienate these interest groups as they are affective at getting the media's attention. And if the crisis does not have significantly affected stakeholders whereby the media can develop stories demonstrating the conflict between the organisation and affected stakeholders, the interest groups will often have an opposing side and argument to that of the organisation which is held to account for the offensive act.

Finally, interest groups are often overlooked in the day to day operations of organisations as an opportunity to collaborate with to develop new directions for the organisation. It is not unusual for discussions with an interest group (that opposes your activities) to highlight thus far missed opportunities. Due to the interest group's knowledge of their subject, they can often assist in helping organisations navigate the problems to explore new opportunities. Interest groups offer far more than just a collective of stoic conservative viewpoints. Often they can be the source of assistance, and sometimes great gains to mutual benefit.

Organisation experiencing the crisis – Last in the list but not least important, the organisation experiencing the crisis is arguably as relevant to the crisis as the affected or aggrieved stakeholders, because without the organisation, there would not be a crisis. (Or at least not until a similar organisation is held to account for an offending act of the same nature). Further focusing the crisis on the organisation is the all too popular blame and punishment attribution of tense situations. As culture based blame orientated publics and news media attribute the offensive act to the organisation, often by proxy the organisation is also the first to be looked at to resolve the undesirable consequences of the crisis. Though it is very unfortunate that the "blame" attribution is generally the first reaction of bystanders (instead of the first reaction being focussed on fixing and prevention), it does initially place the organisation in a dominant media role and focus to take the first steps of precaution and prevention. In other words, when the focus turns to the organisation to attribute blame, there is no reason for the organisation to not seize the opportunity to fix the

[3] The term "slacktivism" is commonly used to describe the activity of individuals who only engage with an issue using social media. Often the only activity by these individuals is limited to the "liking" online content and/or limited to what is viewed as a slack effort.

crisis problem, and ensure that it can never happen again in the organisation and industry. Whilst trying to fix the problem and prevent future problems, not many stakeholders would take issue with the organisation for seeking such productive and positive outcomes from the situation.

3.8 Summary

In summary, trying to solve a crisis without paying much regard to the stakeholders is like performing surgery and disregarding the specifics of the patient. Taking a broadsword approach to stakeholders is a risky and foolhardy way to try to solve a crisis, and will often have a worsening impact. Though it is much easier to disregard stakeholder specifics, it is often the case that disregarding stakeholders creates a crisis.

There are many stakeholder types, relationships, inter-relationships between stakeholders, and other complications. Often not all stakeholders can be readily identified at the onset of a reputational crisis, further complicating crisis containment strategies.

The following chapter provides a brief overview of media in terms of reputational crises. Subsequent chapters discuss different ways of viewing the stakeholder viewpoints, and how to solve already complicated and time poor reputational crises with stakeholders.

Bibliography

Alpanlan, C. M., Green, S. E., & Mitroff, I. (2009). Corporate governance in the context of crisis: Towards a stakeholder theory of crisis management. *Journal of Contingencies & Crisis Management, 17*(1), 38–49.

Benoit, W. L. (1997). Image repair discourse and crisis communication. *Public Relations Review, 23*, 177–186.

BP Claims. (2015, December). *Paid claims list*. Retrieved December 2015, from BP Claims: http://bpclaimshelp.com/paid-claims-list/

Bruce, M., & Soloman, M. R. (2013). Managing for media anarachy: A corporate marketing perspective. *Journal of Marketing Theory and Practice, 21*(3), 307–318.

Coombs, T., & Holladay, S. D. (2014). How publics react to crisis communication efforts: Comparing crisis response reactions. *Journal of Communication Management, 18*(1), 40–57.

Fodor, A., & Stowe, J. (2012). Financial market reactions to a company disaster: The BP case. *Journal of Applied Finance, 1*, 1–16.

Freeman, R. E. (1984). *Strategic management: A stakeholder approach*. Marschfield: Pitman Publishing.

Freeman, R. E. (2004). The stakeholder approach revisited. *Zeitschrift fur Wirtschaft – un Unternnehmensethik, 5*(3), 228–241.

Freeman, R. E., Wicks, A., & Parmar, B. (2004). Stakeholder theory and "The corporate objective revisited". *Organisational Science, 15*(3), 364–369.

Freeman, R. E., Harrison, J. S., Wicks, A. C., Palmar, B. L., & DeColle, S. (2010). *Stakeholder theory: The state of the art*. Cambridge: Cambridge University Press.

Frow, P., & Payne, A. (2011). A stakeholder perspective of the value proposition concept. *European Journal of Marketing, 45*(1), 223–240.

GetUp Australia. (2020). *About GetUp Australia*. Retrieved March 2020, from GetUp Australia. https://www.getup.org.au/about/

International Organisation for Standardization. (2011). *ISO26000 Project Overview*. Retrieved May 2012, from ISO – International Organisation for Standardization. http://www.iso.org/iso/iso_26000_project_overview.pdf

Islam4infidels. (2014). *Buy and return*. Retrieved December 2015, from Islam 4 infidels. http://islam4infidels.com/buy-and-return-halal/

Jaques, T., & Galloway, C. (2012). Coal seam gas in Australia: Can activists be effective from the margins? *Asia Pacific public Relations Journal, 13*(2), 35–44.

Johnston, J. (2015). Loose tweets sink fleets' and other sage advice: Social media governance, policies and guidelines. *Journal of Public Affairs, 15*(2), 175–187.

Key, S. (1999). Toward a new theory of the firm: A critique of stakeholder "theory". *Management Decision, 37*(4), 317–328.

Lerbinger, O. (1997). *The crisis manager: Facing risk and responsibility*. Manwah: Lawrence Erblaum Associates Inc.

Mitchell, R. K., Agle, B. R., & Wood, D. J. (1997). Toward a theory of stakeholder identification and salience. *Academy of Management Review, 22*(4), 853–886.

Moore, H., & Roberts, D. (2013, April 24). *AP Twitter hack causes panic on Wall Street and sends Dow plunging*. Retrieved June 2015, from The Guardian. http://www.theguardian.com/business/2013/apr/23/ap-tweet-hack-wall-street-freefall

Neville, B. A., Bell, S. J., & Whitwell, G. J. (2011). Stakeholder salience revisited: Refining, redefining, and refueling an underdeveloped conceptual tool. *Journal of Business Ethics*, 357–378.

Proctor, R., Vis, F., & Voss, A. (2011, December 8). *Reading the riots: Investigating England's summer of disorder*. Retrieved June 2015, from The Guardian. http://www.theguardian.com/uk/interactive/2011/dec/07/london-riots-twitter

Regester, M., & Larkin, J. (2008). *Risk issues and crisis management*. London: MPG Books Ltd.

Rennie, M. (2019, April 17). *Animal activists charged over protests at Yangan abattoir and Millmerran feedlot*. Retrieved July 9, 2019, from ABC News. https://www.abc.net.au/news/2019-04-17/animal-activists-charged-over-millmerran-yangan-protest/11023422

Schermer, T., & McKenna, B. (2015). Critical analysis of stakeholder theory and corporate social responsibility in social media. In *ANZAM 2015* (pp. 1–14). Queenstown: Australian and New Zealand Academy of Management.

Shirky, C. (2011, January). *The political power of social media*. Retrieved July 2015, from Foreign affairs. https://www.foreignaffairs.org/articles/2010-12-20/political-power-social-media

Sora, K., Soo-Yeon, K., & Sung, K. H. (2014). Fortune 100 companies' Facebook strategies: Corporate ability versus social responsibility. *Journal of Communication Management, 18*(4), 343–362.

Staff and wire reports. (2010, August 23). *Florida real estate agents to share $16 million of BP payout*. Retrieved December 2015, from Herald Tribune. http://www.heraldtribune.com/article/20100824/article/8241018

Tench, R., & Jones, B. (2015). Social media: The Wild West of CSR communications. *Social Responsibility Journal, 11*(2), 290–305.

Tihanyi, L., Graffin, S., & George, G. (2014). Rethinking governance in management research. *Academy of Management Journal, 57*(6), 1535–1543.

Chapter 4
Managing Perceptions – Media in Reputational Crises

Abstract Debating the salience of stakeholders in reputational crises relies on the assumption that media can and will spread news of a reputational crisis. Rarely is image reality based. Instead it is media based. Politicians rely on media to create their image in the minds of their voters. As companies use advertising and other persuasive methods to develop an image, so do interest groups in attempting to gain support for their causes through media audiences.

Underscoring the importance of social media in reputational crisis has become a focal point in reputational crisis theory and strategy, but often ignored are the rules of conduct for engaging with the media, and how media works in reputational crises. Too often the media are not treated as stakeholders but as a non-stakeholder entity. This problem likely comes from the notion that all media has the same objectives. As such, interactions between media and an organisation experiencing a crisis can quickly become problematic as nuances of media interactions and influence can have a significant impact on how reputational crises are reported in the media. This delicate situation is further complicated as other crisis stakeholders can now have a media role through social media.

If a crisis happens in the forest and there is no one to see it, did it happen? The media's role in developing reputational crises, and in supporting various stakeholders, is a key element in reputational crises. In the simplest terms, a reputational crisis is mostly a standoff between an entity (an organisation or person) and stakeholders, and is played out in the mainstream media. And everyone will take sides. This chapter looks at why media is an essential part of reputational crises, and how the popular uptake and changes in social media have changed the landscape of reputational crises and its stakeholders. This followed with a brief look at how media is used persuasively; in particular how powerful framing is and has been used in popular culture during times of war. The remainder of this chapter looks at the main dynamics that are at play during press conferences for reputational crises, and the not so often considered problems faced when making media statements during a reputational crisis.

T. Schermer, *Reputational Crises Unspun*, https://doi.org/10.1007/978-981-16-5130-4_4

The role of media is arguably central to reputational crises as it bridges the gap between stakeholders and the organisation, and the media develops a perception of the offending act that leads to the crisis. Continuing with analogy of 'if a tree falls in the forest, and there is no one around, does it make a sound?' It does if the media has somehow recorded it and distributed it. And if the recording is from an angle that illuminates the sensationalism of the tree crashing, it will appeal to a large audience.

In crisis communication research the media has not been a significant focus. The main area of research of media in crisis communication centres on the framing of the media messages, but generally does not engage with the news media industry or the production of news media. The following section discusses the role of the media in reputational crises, focusing on perceptions and the ever increasingly important social media.

4.1 The Reach of Media

As "perceptions are more important than reality" (Benoit, 1997, p. 178), for a reputational crisis to be significant enough to affect public interest or support, it must receive significant media coverage. Public image is not necessarily, and oftentimes not reality based (Benoit, 1995, 1997; Schultz, 2004). With the exception of very a mere handful, the public is informed by media (Schultz, 2004; Louw, 2005). "The media provide contact with social reality and give people access particular to those events which they cannot watch with their own eyes, first hand" (Schultz, 2004, pp. 90–91). Schultz (2004, p. 89) states "As media use becomes an integral part of private and social life, the media's definition of reality amalgamates with the social definition of reality". Thus when viewing reputation management, through the lens provided by media, the sum image of the entity's managed and reported reputation is often the only accessible source presented to external stakeholders and society by which to understand the crisis. By means of Freemans's definition of stakeholder as anyone who can be affected by a company, or anyone who can affect the company; the reputational crisis stakeholder is anyone who can affect or be affected by the crisis. Therefore any consumer of media pertaining to the crisis may be a crisis stakeholder. The notion that media is critical in reputational crises is supported by Schultz's (2004) suggestion that the reality provided by the media is of significant importance as "media technologies extend the natural limits of human communication capacities. Human communication is limited in terms of space, time and expressiveness; the media serve to bridge the spatial gap" (Schultz, 2004, p. 88).

The role of traditional news media organisations is to create content for its publication or broadcast, to create revenue from advertising between content. The news media regularly use reputational crises as sources of content, playing a significant role in the duration and impact of the reputational crisis (Lerbinger, 1997). The role of media in reputational crises should not be understated, as without media, company stakeholders would likely not be aware of a reputational crisis, and thereby those stakeholders would not review the relationship with the company. Furthermore the media plays a role in framing the news stories as a means to classify a crisis, which can impact the longevity of the crisis (Lerbinger, 1997).

Some of the more contemporary research engages with internet based media content, however the majority of that focusses on internet based media developed by large media corporations. Only recently some research and literature in crisis communication is centred on social media, despite social media rapidly becoming relevant to reputational crises. The next section discusses social media in this context.

4.2 Social Media

Since the internet became more commonly used in the early 2000's, various platforms have been popular for social networking. Early popular platforms focussed on direct (pier to pier) communications and had limited facilities for sharing content with multiple persons or interacting with groups. Since then the emphasis of social networking platform design has become focussed on user friendly tools and making it easier to disseminate information.

Social networking platforms have evolved to allow for one person to engage with members of groups or collectives in various modes, including 1 to many, many to 1, and many to many. The current forerunners of social media platforms in the western hemisphere are Facebook, Twitter, and Instagram. Each of these platforms allows a single user to engage with sources often regardless if the user is a subscriber to the source, or linked to the source. The social media platforms also allow users to comment and publish text and/or graphics of their choosing. These changes have removed the once secular nature of online social networking communications, and allow for the dissemination of information and engagement with individuals and groups whilst the user is not necessarily a member of the same groups and viewpoints.

For reputational crises this means that any user can engage with most groups, and bring complaints or issues to the attention of many social media users, often without the obstructions of gatekeepers, and publish that information to thousands of users within a few seconds. For example, any Facebook user may post a complaint or concern on a store's Facebook page and get the attention of thousands of other users. Such a posting may come to the attention of various stakeholders such as the store's suppliers, other customers, authorities, competitors, and sometimes news media companies.

The following section discusses the nature of social media, and how the relationships in social media have evolved to change the nature of stakeholders and news media.

Throughout the last decade collective action groups have formed on social media, with some of these groups achieving significant success in furthering the development of their respective causes (GetUp Australia, 2020; Shirky, 2011) Such successes inspired a proliferation of social media action groups seeking to influence social, economic and political agendas in corporations and governments alike (Shirky, 2011). The manner in which social activists and corporate stakeholders can employ social media to further their causes is currently an understudied area, as most corporations still struggle to manage these crisis stakeholders.

The proliferation of social media use and engagement by corporations is being closely followed by an increasing volume of academic research seeking to understand and manage these new media platforms (Johnston, 2015; Coombs & Holladay, 2014) The rapid increase in social media use in society has left corporations inadequately prepared to engage with this new medium (Bruce & Soloman, 2013). Because social media is by nature established in the public domain, each entity, be it a large company or single person, is represented individually and with equal voice as any other entity (Bruce & Soloman, 2013). This contrasts with the disparity in traditional news media in how individuals and larger companies and organisations are represented in other society and media. For example, the physical presence of a large corporation in traditional media is often congruent with the economic power of that organisation, as they can purchase more advertising space and/or time. Whereas an individual in society most often can't afford to spend large sums of money in the media pursue their agenda. In the social media environment, each participant, be it a large corporation or individual person, has the same authority, rights and limitations (Bruce & Soloman, 2013).

The hybrid nature of social media, as a tool for communication with a large number of participants both sending and receiving communications, places it outside the parameters of traditional information distribution services and traditional news media (Bruce & Soloman, 2013). This unique aspect of information distribution not only challenges the traditional information distribution models of news media, but also included with that is the accountability aspect that is relied upon in the traditional news media. Traditional news media was, and still is, accountable to the owners of the news media organisation, news industry ethics associations, government legislation, and civil actions such as defamation. In contrast, social media users are not accountable to anyone, and through anonymity, such as fake social media accounts (Tench & Jones, 2015), can more easily avoid defamation claims. The social media model places information dissemination into the hands of anyone without any requirement of accuracy, media ethics, or accountability (Bruce & Soloman, 2013). Hence social media can and does carry with it a greater risk of spreading unreliable and incorrect information. Examples of unreliable social media ranges from the hacked AFP twitter account stating the White House was attacked (Moore & Roberts, 2013), to claims of riots in a London burger restaurant (Proctor et al., 2011). The implications that follow from such lack of accountability and responsibility, combined with the potential of an individual or small interest group effectively developing a greater social media audience than a corporation, is a concern for the traditional methods of stakeholder engagement in crisis communication and management. Although corporations can hire multiple staff to manage their social media profile, social activist groups can through the use of many supporters and fake profiles, often and easily diffuse and/or annul a corporation's attempts to manage its profile and crisis communication strategies.

The above section provides an insight into the difficulties faced by corporations and crisis communicators operating in the social media environment. The body of literature on social media's implications, opportunities, and management in crisis communication is currently an understudied area, evidenced by the rapidly growing volume of research contributions to the field.

In summary, media bridges the "spatial gap" (Schultz, 2004, p. 88) between receivers and senders of information. For reputational crisis communication purposes social media differs significantly from traditional media and has the challenges of:

- Presence of one organisation on social media can easily have the same influence as a single individual on social media;
- Mass communication through social media can mean there are as many senders of communication as there are receivers of communication;
- Any communications may be based on unreliable and/or incorrect information.

4.3 Framing and Meaning Makers – History

Before Gutenberg developed his printing press, public opinion has been formed through the media. Be it through a town crier, stone tablets distributed to houses of religious worship, or just a vocal member of the community. Since the days of Gutenberg's printing press, it has become easier and more efficient to develop public opinions and meaning. During the past century, many news media organisation were developed, and in the latter part of the century, most were acquired by large media companies, leading to a more singular voice developing meaning through the media across the globe. The development of the internet meant that the traditional news channels were able develop public opinions on all subjects in an instant across the globe.

Meaning making is well documented and researched throughout academic literature, and often cited by anti-establishment groups as proof of propaganda, political manipulation, and financial manipulation. The method of using propaganda to antagonise the public's opinion about issues, and to create a public sensitivity on specific issues using a specific focal point, often gets used by interest groups, and organisations alike, to gain support for certain issues in the public arena.

4.3.1 Propaganda for War

Meaning making engages with the concepts of framing the meaning of things. That is to say, stories are developed to give certain meaning and to further push the public's interests in particular directions. For instance, when former US President, George W. Bush and his supporters pushed for the invasion of Iraq, it was done so through the media. In this, the media was given photographic and video evidence to support to the invasion, was well as specific documents, which when summarily viewed by the public, would galvanise the arguments for invading Iraq. To ensure that President Bush was developing public opinion in the right direction, he formed the White House Iraq Group, or WHIG (Wikipedia-WHIG, 2018). President Bush realised that he needed the public support for such an invasion and established WHIG for that purpose.

Managing the public support for war using media is a well-established practice. Before the Second World War, Adolf Hitler's right hand man and Minister for Propaganda, Joseph Goebbels, studied the practices of how the English had managed the public relations during the First World War (Louw, 2005, p. 213; Goebbels, 1939). Goebbels went on to develop Hitler's powerful military might with strong public support, developed through the media. Goebbels stated "If the English want a fight with Germany, they will not be fighting the Führer or a small ruling circle, but a united nation of 80 million Germans… It must face the hard and unchangeable facts" (Goebbels, 1939). Goebbels polarised the public by inferring that the English wanted to fight all the Germans, not just Hitler. Naturally for Germans hearing this, they would assume that the English were the protagonists of war. Furthermore, the strategy forced the Germans to align themselves not just to each other, but also with Hitler who was to protect them.

Goebbels wasn't the last to use the polarisation of stakeholders. Former United States President, George W. Bush, famously polarised stakeholders in *the war against terrorism* with his slogan "you are either with us or against us" (CNN, 2001). This method is effective in addressing the public to galvanise support. In this, the only option is to support George Bush's agenda, as anyone else would be branded a supporter of terrorists. This alienation of stakeholders who do not give wholesale support to a cause effectively marginalises them not just as an affront to the cause, but also to any stakeholder who supports the cause. This method of alienation can easily erupt into a reputational crisis as large numbers of stakeholders may agree to the original premise; that terrorism is bad and must be fought. However, most stakeholders would have different viewpoints on how to fight terrorism, and would not support the en masse invasions of other sovereign countries (Pincus, 1985).

This is an effective strategic method of framing and can quickly lead to the fragmentation of stakeholder groups and lead to a reputational crisis. For example, in recent years a social movement successfully brought about a media focus on factory farmed eggs, and promoted free range eggs. Billboards, newspapers, and television advertising showed images of three chickens stuck in a cage the size of an A4 piece of paper. Many more consumers started buying free range eggs in the supermarket. That is, until a cataclysmic fragmentation of stakeholders of the egg industry. Some animal rights groups had very different views on what was considered free range. Nearly immediately, some egg farmers saw it as a chance to promote how well their chickens lived on acres of fields. This of course alienated other egg farmers who thought an open air chicken coup meant free range. The animal rights groups seized on this media coverage, which led to the main supermarkets being asked what their idea of free range really meant. Finally, after much media and nearly 2 years, the industry has settled down and have made tentative standards to determine what are and aren't free range eggs. This example shows how quickly stakeholders became fragmented and reputational crises erupted for many, when the framing of the free range message was left open ended.

4.4 Presenting to the Media and Social Psychology

Despite and perhaps because of our intuition, we generally tend to avoid trying to understand exactly what we feel and why we feel a certain way about something. Most people enjoy the simplicity of "just because" and following their intuition. Psychology research offers us a reasonable insight into both this phenomena and how reputational crisis communication can matter. The next sections discuss a number of social psychology concepts that are relevant in reputational crises.

4.4.1 In the Media Scrum – Legitimacy Gap Theory

Using legitimacy gap theory in reputational crisis communication allows us to better understand the legitimacy of crisis communication statements. If a statement is made by an entity, and that entity is not perceived to be a legitimate speaker or authority on the matter, than the statement will be at best ignored, but most likely the statement will be scrutinised for further problems which will in turn be developed into extra media stories that will be related to the crisis, thereby increasing the impacts of the crisis or extending the crisis.

The basic premise of legitimacy gap theory is illustrated with a study by Heath (1997). Heath's paper describes how the racial tensions between black and white Americans were not improved by the media statements of black leaders. Although contemporary politically correct thinking means that we consider the statements of a black leader to be as legitimate as those of a white leader, this was not the case during the last centuries. Heath was found that statements made by now highly acclaimed and considered influential black leaders including Martin Luther King, did nothing to influence the white audiences for which most of the news media was developed. Although Martin Luther King appealed to the values of white society, to develop a discourse more conducive to resolving racial discrimination, it had little effect. The very problem he was trying to address was also the problem which stopped his audience from accepting his views. That is to say, even though he was talking about the values of white people and correctly relating to their values, he failed to have an impact on the white audience because as a black person he was seen as an outsider who had no business telling them about their values.

Similarly, a CEO arriving at a disaster in a helicopter wearing perfectly polished boots is not considered to have legitimate association to those working in the disaster who are covered head to toe in mud and struggling to stay on top of the deluge. If the leader would instead turn up in the same clothes as the workers, and genuinely pitch in as a team member, then the team would relate to him, and accept his legitimacy. These examples underscore what is often a problem for CEO's and heads of government when trying to deal with the general public.

A political example of the same obstacles is found in a former Australian politician. The meteoric rise to political success by a previously unknown mayoral candidate could be attributed to his simple campaign to relate to his audience. Instead of wearing a full suit and tie in his mayoral election campaign, the candidate donned some work clothes and started filling potholes in streets in the city. His constituents loved that he was working hard, but also that they could relate to him as one of their own. His legitimacy was based on working hard which was an important attribute in that society. Interestingly when the same man later became Premier and appointed a barely 30 year old man with only 6 months law experience as the Attorney General of the state. The Attorney General's lack of experience became a focus point when tough new laws were introduced by him. The courts, and subsequently some of the legal fraternity of the state rallied against the Attorney General and some considered him as a boy-man who had no idea and no experience. His legitimacy was under attack because his broader reputation was based on little more than a political appointment. Numerous discussions were held which were resulted with a media photo opportunity showing the young Attorney General shaking hands with the senior members of the legal fraternity. In the sense of the media, he had developed his reputation. However, the means of doing so and his nominal experience did little to create a loyalty and support from the legal fraternity. This provided the perfect opportunity for the opposing political party to seek support from the legal fraternity for the next election. The legitimacy of a person going against the status quo is critical in gaining acceptance from the audience.

4.4.2 Media and Friends – In-Group and Out-Group Behaviours

Social psychology research is focussed on the interactions between individuals, groups and society. The multitude of situations that we find ourselves in daily are too many to describe, thus often research seeks to find the common aspects of those many situations, and focus on those aspects to try to determine some form of pattern.

In/out group behaviours refers to how individuals or groups deals and interact with other individuals or groups that do not share the same situation, beliefs or values. For example, a class room full of students is an in-group and the teacher is outside of that group as he/she is not a student. In such situation, the teacher will be considered as an outsider and his/her judgements will be considered to be different by the group of students. In the class room situation this is necessary to allow the teacher to assert authority and ensure that teacher is listened to. If the teacher was considered equal to the students, by the students, then it would be difficult for the teacher's voice to be heard amongst the cacophony of the student's banter. However, in the classroom situation, the teacher can rely on the transferred authority to him/her. This authority is in the form of other teachers, the school and is endorsed by society and parental figures. Thus if one tries to transpose this scenario so that a CEO is listened to in a reputational crises, the CEO must have some form of legitimacy of authority as the teacher does from the social institution that is the school. Unfortunately for the lone standing CEO, the lone CEO does not enjoy the benefits of transferred authority from any social institution, so the CEO must earn the respect of the audience in an organic manner through gaining legitimacy as an authority.

Outsider in Society
A common misconception amongst corporate leaders is that they have a position of authority in mainstream society, similar as they enjoy a position of authority in the company of which they are in charge. In the company, the CEO is part of the in-group and has the authority of the entire company. In this situation, the authority of the CEO is attributed to the position held by the CEO, as opposed to authority attributed CEO personally. However, in mainstream society, the CEO has no more legitimacy of authority than the average person in that society. Oftentimes CEO's can easily miscomprehend their corporate authority to be legitimate in society to be similar to that of a head of state, president or prime minister. When a CEO does not recognise this misnomer, the CEO is more likely to reduce his/her authority through attempting to gain legitimacy through illegitimate means, as the society has not subjugated itself to the CEO's authority. This misstep can easily increase the damage to a corporation's image during a reputational crisis, and in the worst case, exacerbate the reputational crisis as the CEO could easily be framed as being too big for their boots, arrogant and presumptive, and offensive to society.

Outside in the Media Scrum
The in-group out-group issue also manifests itself in similar circumstances, whereby the CEO might believe that he/she is part of the collegial crowd of news media staff who are seeking an interview. In a media conference, the CEO does have the legitimacy of authority, but only inside the media conference. That is to say, the news media personnel who make up the group of people have voluntarily given authority to the CEO as the person at the front to be in charge during the conference. However the legitimacy of authority ends as soon as the press conference is over, and the CEO remains as an out-group to the news media personnel. Any notion of being part of the collegial fraternity of the news media is often met with disdain and distrust. For example, the CEO is in charge of hundreds (if not thousands of staff) and the news reporter has no staff; the CEO earns millions and the reporter earns thousands; the CEO does as he/she deems fit, and the reporter has a hierarchy above him/her who give constant instructions on everything. This is likely to make the reporter feel as though the CEO is privileged and can lead the reporter to feel resentful, influencing the reporter to find another sensational angle to the reputational crisis and write another story.

4.4.3 Outsider Losing Control of the Narrative

The BP Deepwater Horizon oil spill provides another example of in-out group behaviours and how these impact news media reporting during a reputational crisis. In this crisis the technical specialists that BP used as their spokesperson at times during the crisis, made the news media audience feel inadequate as the briefing was too technical to be understood and translated by the news media reporters. This type of alienation by the technical specialists made the news media reporters ignore what the specialist was trying to communicate, and instead they reported what they felt was important. Oftentimes, this type of scenario means that the company is losing control of the story, and the news media will sensationalise it as much as it can to sell more news. Most likely, the company will be labelled as arrogant as a result, and the crisis will further escalate.

The preferred method for disseminating technical information in a reputational crisis is by a non-technical representative, who has had the technical information explained and deconstructed to them by a technical expert. This then allows the non-technical representative to explain and deconstruct the information to the news media in the same manner, but without the technical jargon and complicated details. This preferred method also means that the company representative can be selected from a larger pool of staff, and it allows for the selection of a representative who is far more likely to be considered in-group rather than out-group to the news media personnel.

Bibliography

Benoit, W. L. (1995). *Accounts, excuses, and apologies: A theory of image restoration strategies.* Albany: State University of New York Press.

Benoit, W. L. (1997). Image repair discourse and crisis communication. *Public Relations Review, 23*, 177–186.

Bruce, M., & Soloman, M. R. (2013). Managing for media anarachy: A corporate marketing perspective. *Journal of Marketing Theory and Practice, 21*, 307–318.

CNN. (2001, November 6). *You are either with us or against us.* Retrieved November 2018, from CNN.com. http://edition.cnn.com/2001/US/11/06/gen.attack.on.terror/

Coombs, T., & Holladay, S. D. (2014). How publics react to crisis communication efforts: Comparing crisis response reactions. *Journal of Communication Management, 18*(1), 40–57.

GetUp Australia. (2020). *About GetUp Australia.* Retrieved March 2020, from GetUp Australia. https://www.getup.org.au/about/

Goebbels, J. (1939, June 24). *Children with their hands chopped off.* Retrieved November 2018, from Calvin College. https://research.calvin.edu/german-propaganda-archive/goeb27.htm

Heath, R. L. (1997). *Strategic issues management: Organisations and public policy challenges.* Thousand Oaks: Sage.

Johnston, J. (2015). Loose tweets sink fleets' and other sage advice: Social media governance, policies and guidelines. *Journal of Public Affairs, 15*(2), 175–187.

Lerbinger, O. (1997). *The crisis manager: Facing risk and responsibility.* Manwah: Lawrence Erblaum Associates Inc.

Louw, E. (2005). *The media and political process.* London: Sage.

Moore, H., & Roberts, D. (2013, April 24). *AP Twitter hack causes panic on Wall Street and sends Dow plunging*. Retrieved June 2015, from The Guardian. http://www.theguardian.com/business/2013/apr/23/ap-tweet-hack-wall-street-freefall

Pincus, T. H. (1985). A crisis parachute: Helping stock prices have a soft landing. *Journal of Business Strategy, 6*(4), 32–38.

Proctor, R., Vis, F., & Voss, A. (2011, December 8). *Reading the riots: Investigating England's summer of disorder*. Retrieved June 2015, from The Guardian. http://www.theguardian.com/uk/interactive/2011/dec/07/london-riots-twitter

Schultz, W. (2004). Reconstructing mediatization as an analytical concept. *European Journal of Communication, 19*(1), 87–101.

Shirky, C. (2011, January). *The political power of social media*. Retrieved July 2015, from Foreign affairs. https://www.foreignaffairs.org/articles/2010-12-20/political-power-social-media

Tench, R., & Jones, B. (2015). Social media: The Wild West of CSR communications. *Social Responsibility Journal, 11*(2), 290–305.

Wikipedia-WHIG. (2018, April). *White House Iraq Group*. Retrieved November 2018, from Wikipedia. https://en.wikipedia.org/wiki/White_House_Iraq_Group

Part II

This second part of the book explores how reputational crises can be understood better, managed better, and communicated better. It provides a more practical approach to solving reputational crises, and preventing reputational crises. The final chapter is a multiple choice quiz which is followed with detailed answers to explain the ethos on how to avoid and fix reputational crises.

Chapter 5
Crisis Communication and Management Challenges

Abstract Despite reputational crises being a highly visible problem in society through making up a significant part of everyday news media coverage, solutions to reputational crises and prevention strategies are mostly incomplete.

Reputational crises and post crisis reviews are studied by industry and academia with the objective of solving and preventing crises. Yet authors of popularly used and cited reputational crisis theory, and meta-studies alike, regularly conclude that extant theories are insufficient for dealing with every type of reputational crisis.

This chapter reviews the more common obstacles and problematic strategies in reputational crisis theory and strategy, finding the common thread of these is the company centric approach to solving reputational crises often limits effective crisis resolution and prevention. The ethos of solving reputational crises for the sake of benefiting of the company experiencing the crisis is often a direct affront to crisis stakeholder's wellbeing and preventing future crises. Crisis communication research and practice seems to be more about defending a position rather than rather than seeking to understand what was considered wrong with that position, and then working together to fix the problem and prevent similar future events.

This chapter reviews the challenges in contemporary crisis communication and management literature, and shows how these challenges have been instrumental in not effectively dealing with, and solving, reputational crises. The use and common understanding of contemporary stakeholder theory is reviewed in terms of reputational crises and highlighted as a real obstacle for effectively managing and communicating through reputational crises. Next, the attribution of blame in crises is looked as another obstacle to dealing with crisis stakeholder successfully. This chapter is then summarized as a platform for the subsequent chapter which looks at different ways to solve crises, without the encumbrances of ineffective strategies, theories, and practice.

T. Schermer, *Reputational Crises Unspun*, https://doi.org/10.1007/978-981-16-5130-4_5

Contemporary crisis communication, crisis management strategies, and theories are fraught with obstacles. Including;

- Stakeholder theory is often used in theory and practice as though it is a ready to go tool that instantly fits into any situation. Though Freeman, the founder of the contemporary stakeholder theory, is making significant efforts to improve stakeholder theory because nearly all existing theory and practice is based on the problematic stakeholder theory in the most simplified form.
- Crises are caused by an offensive act, but we have very limited knowledge of how offensive acts work to incite stakeholders to action. Some researchers have started several different paths to understanding the offensive act better, but mostly they have employed the status quo company centred formats, which do little to genuinely understanding the stakeholder's viewpoint, thus making it near impossible to understand the "offensiveness".
- Anyone can create media. Society, industry, and researchers are all working frantically in many directions, coming up with many different results and strategies. Though often lacking is the insight that social media is still in its infancy, and as such is rapidly growing and more importantly; rapidly evolving. Thus to forever define the media landscape now, would be presumptive and likely exclude significant future research, understanding, and changes in the social media landscape.
- A reputational crisis solved is not an issue fixed. This is possibly the most perplexing dilemma as nearly all literature considers a crisis solved as a complete success. It feels a bit like putting out a house fire, and then leaving the matches in idle hands. It is little wonder interest groups and afflicted stakeholders seek legislative changes following a crisis.

Though most academics and some industry professionals will take issue with these statements, the evidence is everywhere. Reputational crises are here to stay, are becoming more frequent, and many are not fixing the cause of the problems. It does appear that most crises tend to burn out due to a lack of fuel, rather than good strategies and insight.

Some of the largest and well-resourced companies (Facebook, BP) and even the most powerful public relations company (Cambridge Analytica) were unable to stave off their own reputational crises. When the public, shareholders, legislators, and other stakeholders punish an organisation for offensive behaviour, the issues remain largely unaddressed.

5.1 Examples of Issues Not Fixed

Cambridge Analytica – When Cambridge Analytica was caught out using data to influence voting, the company tried to go into battle with its accusers. Eventually Cambridge Analytica closed its doors. All the politicians, legislators, and the public slept peacefully thereafter. Because everyone knew the evil was finished. Then everyone went online to complain about it. Then they went to the shops with their loyalty cards and felt better about getting a good bargain and completely forgot about Cambridge Analytica. Of course the irony here is that Cambridge Analytica was pretty much held to account for doing what a lot of companies do today; they collected data and used it to further their own cause. The supermarket, frequented by those people who now sleep well, still collects your loyalty program data and pitches everything to suit what they believe you should buy. Your local politician still takes every bit of voter data he is legally entitled to, in an effort to work out who you are, and pitch a political message to suit your needs so he can get your vote. In other words, even though Cambridge Analytica is gone, the data security and data use problems are growing incrementally every day. The Cambridge Analytica crisis is over. The issue has not been fixed.

Top Gear – When Jeremy Clarkson offended the social mores of his television show, Top Gear, the organisation simply dumped Clarkson and his co-stars. However, as a television show, Top Gear had a massive audience and was worth a fortune, so another station simply picked up the show and made a fortune with it since then. Clarkson's issues were never addressed on the show and everything continued as it did before.

British Petroleum (BP) failed miserably during its Deepwater Horizon crisis. Much research not long after showed that BP managed the media badly by using engineers to talk about what was happening. Many journalists either lost interest in the engineer's rhetoric, or simply gave up trying to translate engineering talk to their news media consumers. Two years later BP advertised for a crisis communications manager for its Australian operations, with the minimum requirement being engineering qualifications. The company suffered a 58% drop (Sabet et al., 2012) in share price (US$108 billion) during the Deepwater Horizon crisis, and still follow the same path with crisis communication, and possibly strategy.

These few are not many examples. There are thousands of examples every year. But these few are some of the world's largest and most profitable companies, who thereby have the most resources and should by that reason alone, be able to acquire whatever they need to help get them out of the crisis and the fix the issues. Even more tragic; as some of the largest companies in the world today they had the opportunity to lead every other company in how to deal with crisis and subsequent problems. How to not just save their shareholders billions, and save their stakeholders from an undeserved bad situation, but also how be proactive and fix problems when their reputation is in question.[1]

It is an impossible task to learn to know exactly what each and every stakeholder wants, and it is counterintuitive to dealing with a time pressurized crisis. However a lot of companies seem to be doing the total opposite; that is assuming that if they

[1] Companies use the most sophisticated labs to create products and social psychologists to improve their brand perception all the time, and then market sample their products after spending millions on research, and yet in a crisis, suddenly executives believe they have perfect and instant solutions and instantly understand their stakeholders perfectly, albeit from a company perspective.

only just *say* what they *believe* their stakeholders want to hear, that the crisis is solved forever.

Moving away from the practical examples of failures in crisis communication strategy, the academic literature has many challenges as well.

5.2 Obstacles in Stakeholder Theory for Crisis Communication

The predominant focus of crisis communication research is centred on stakeholders; how stakeholders come into existence, which messages work best for them, how they actually react to boycotts and strikes and negative media, and so forth. All these ideas are well intentioned; however most of them take the basic premise of Freeman's (1984) stakeholder theory for granted, even though Freeman himself has worked hard since his original publication to remove focus from solely trying to benefit the corporation. The notion that the corporation is at the centre of everything and its stakeholders surround the corporation, is great for use in basic theory use because it is so simple and takes very little into account.

If we were to view a stakeholder map during a reputational crisis, the picture would look very different. It would include many stakeholder alliances, and through the sheer influence of stakeholders and their respective alliances, place the stakeholders at the centre of the crisis stakeholder map and the organisation on the inner circle, together with legislators, media, interest groups, and so forth. Furthermore, in crises where there have been fatalities, the families and bereaved would most likely be at the centre of the stakeholder map, with the organisation struggling to develop a respectful image and all the while trying to work its way back to the centre of the crisis and media attention.

5.3 Obstacles Resulting from Attribution Theory for Crisis Communication

Where the crisis communication literature focussed on stakeholder responses to image restoration strategies and crisis communication strategies, it regularly employs Weiner's (1986) attribution theory to engage with the constructs. In the greater context of seeking to make the connection between crisis communication messaging effectiveness and how these are received, attribution theory does fit quite well. Unfortunately, the basic assumption of attribution is about the stakeholder's perception of the organisation experiencing the crisis. This means that the focus is based on the basic assumption that if a company has done something wrong, the most common response in today's society is to attribute blame. And in our cultural constructs, we have been taught that if you are blamed for something, often the most popular response is offense or defence.[2] This polarity of choices is somewhat counterintuitive to working together to solve the problem that created the crisis, because both offensive and defensive strategies are mostly about defending a position, rather than seeking to understand what was considered wrong with that position, and then working together to fix the problem and prevent similar future events.

The development of image restoration strategies are mostly the result of much deductive research by Benoit. And although the strategies Benoit offered are a true reflection of history by means of the case studies Benoit used, they are arguably not congruent with a collaborative stakeholder relationship to solve an issue and prevent similar future events. At least nine of fourteen of Benoit's strategies are common to combative or adversarial communications. Outside of those nine strategies, Benoit does list accident and good intentions (though under the category of evading responsibility) and compensation under the "reducing the offensiveness" category. In addition Benoit lists corrective action and mortification last, and both as their own category and strategy. However these last two strategies are not so often represented in the research literature (this might be because they are rarely practiced in real crises) or because they require more event specific information (for testing in lab conditions, denial is easy to simulate, but corrective action may require more imagination to simulate as a crisis response). Unfortunately crisis communication research is not rich in content of corrective action and mortification.

5.4 Shortcomings of Crisis Communication Focus

In summary, crisis communication research is about finding the most effective message to reduce negative impacts of a reputational crisis. However this is mostly about reducing the negative impact on the organisation that has committed the offending act. It appears there is no research on the effective crisis communication strategies that focus on reducing the negative impact on the stakeholders first; whilst without those affected stakeholders, there often wouldn't be a crisis at all.

Arguably crisis communication is just about that; communicating in a crisis, and not about crisis fixing strategies. However the crisis communication research and practice literature is nearly entirely centred on what happens if we say we will do a certain thing. Furthermore, the literature is centred on what is communicated, and thus there should be at least some focus on the actual crisis strategies as these form

[2] The offence and defence options are represented in Benoit's image restoration strategies which include simple denial, shifting blame, provocation, defeasibility, accident, bolstering, minimization, differentiation, and transcendence.

the basis of what is communicated. For instance, the idea of communication typologies as used by Benoit begs the question why Benoit and others have not engaged with the idea of using 'best practice' as an apologia strategy? In the case of Benoit (1995), he based his strategies on an extensive array of excuses and accounts used in a variety of situations, and possibly Benoit's research did not uncover common usage of 'best practice' as a strategy. This is not to say that Benoit's list of accounts and excuses is not extensive or well researched, but it seems naive to accept that the first (and most notable) literature on apologia and accounts cannot be improved upon. Unless we continue to revaluate not just our current way of thinking but also our long accepted knowledge, we are not likely to develop, grow, or evolve in a manner which is beneficial.

5.5 Most Companies Want Free Media, But Not During a Crisis

Ironically some companies have found themselves in the hot water that is a reputational crisis after some stunts as attempts to get free publicity. Typically companies and public relations firms try to get as much free media as possible, but in a reputational crisis they shy away from the media attention. The sudden and aggressive onset of media attention during a crisis is often more than the average communication department is capable of handling well. Thus the most effective preventative measure is to prepare crisis media release templates ready for use should a crisis occur.

It is helpful to work together with the media to manage the company image that is being created in the media. If you refuse to work with the media, they will develop their own content and it will likely not be favourable to the company, simply because that doesn't entice the media audience (should you choose to work with the media, the Media Statements and instruction chapter of this book will be helpful).

The news media is interested in developing a story about the crisis, but do not necessarily want to demonise the organisation experiencing the crisis, if there is a better way to tell the story. The media's staff will want the story quickly, smoothly, and factually. If you can provide them with the story in a manner that fits these criteria they are less likely to reframe the story, and not give your organisation an overly negative portrayal.

Essentially the story will come to a close over the course of time, and there will be a reason that explains why the crisis has ended. If at all possible, it would serve well to steer the media towards that reason and to integrate this reason throughout the crisis.

Bibliography

Benoit, W. L. (1995). *Accounts, excuses, and apologies: A theory of image restoration strategies*. Albany: State University of New York Press.

Freeman, R. E. (1984). *Strategic management: A stakeholder approach*. Marschfield: Pitman Publishing.

Sabet, S., Cam, M., & Heaney, R. (2012). Sharemarket reaction to the BP oil spill and the US government moratorium on exploration. *Australian Journal of Management, 37*(1), 61–76.

Weiner, B. (1986). *An attributional theory of motivation and emotion*. New York: Springer.

Chapter 6
Thinking Differently: Reputational Crises Resituated

Abstract This review of reputational crisis literature and practice finds that the challenges in contemporary crisis communication and strategy are predominantly borne out a company centric stakeholder model. Reputational crises require stakeholders to exist, for without stakeholders no action would be considered offensive and thus not develop into a reputational crisis. Yet most literature fails to acknowledge that stakeholders are salient to crises. Although for the purpose of the company's survival, the crisis must be brought to an end and avoided in future, the method of successfully accomplishing this must at least in part be through the crisis stakeholders' viewpoints. To accomplish this more holistic solution to solving reputational crises, the focus should be removed from the company and given to the crisis instead. This change of focus fits within the more recent revisions of stakeholder theory and through providing a more egalitarian approach to the company and its stakeholders, makes room not only for apologia to be more effective and genuine, but also allows us to see crisis stakeholders as salient to the crisis as the company is salient to the crisis. This strategy may also be more conducive to preventing future reputational crises.

This chapter begins with a review of what the offending element of a reputational crisis really is, and how stakeholders view it. Building on the overview of stakeholder empathy discussed in previous chapters, it takes a closer look at how stakeholders feel (and why we should be considerate of them) is explained providing a refreshing insight into developing genuine empathy for reputational crisis stakeholders. This provides a new look at apologising and aids in how we view making reparations. This followed with looking at stakeholder viewpoints, and questioning the worth of attributing blame. The remainder of this chapter proposes taking a positive and proactive approach to stakeholder theory, and using it to solve reputational crises. In this, the 'implied rules of conduct' of how modern societies expect organisations to act, provides a more holistic idea blueprint on reputational crises.

This second part is dedicated to how we can view reputational crises differently, and using new and different viewpoints combined with collaborative stakeholder

T. Schermer, *Reputational Crises Unspun*, https://doi.org/10.1007/978-981-16-5130-4_6

strategies to fix reputational crises, to avoid them in future, and to improve industry standards.

6.1 What Is Considered an Offensive Act?

A reputational crisis comes about when an organisation is held to account for having committed an offending act (Benoit, 1997). It seems nearly all crisis communication and mitigation strategy texts skip the "offensive" part and move straight to saying something to reduce the offensiveness. Out of context, this does not make sense. It seems a bit like being placed in front of a judge for robbing a bank, and instead of being concerned with the law, just telling the judge "I'm sorry I broke the law, but I really just wanted to get ahead financially. My wife (the shareholder) to whom I am accountable, demands a certain amount of financial growth every year, and I was just doing my best". Needless to say, the judge would throw the book at you and remind you that we all live in a shared society and environment. Perhaps it is that society is not perceived to be as insightful as a judge, or maybe many think that a single person robbing a bank really should be punished more than a large corporation. A notable anomaly in this example is the bank robber broke an actual law, whereas often corporations do not break a law, but the offensive act still is incongruent with how we expect others to behave in our shared social and ecological environments. This then raises the question; what is offensive?

The answer to this question is difficult to synthesise as we need to we take into account different types of societies. In some developing nations, societies still work together every day to improve the prosperity of the society, tribes, or families. In these societies there are different codes of conduct than in western capitalist societies where everyone is focussed on getting as much as they can for themselves. An organisation could find itself in a reputational crisis through simply taking much more than they are expected to take, albeit within the confines of the law (Stefanova, 2001).

Geert Hofstede studied different cultures around the world when he was employed by IBM. The company had branches in many countries and Hofstede was able to survey some 100,000 staff to find similarities and differences between the different cultures (Jandt, 2010). Unfortunately Hofstede's research, although extensive and well regarded, provides little to no insight into distilling and defining the idea of "offensive" as used by Benoit to describe an unpopular act that leads to a crisis.

Swapping the lens from viewing society as a large group to looking at individuals and what is most important to individual people, often the focus lands on human values research by Milton Rokeach (Rokeach, 1973). Rokeach performed many human values surveys of a number of decades. In this, Rokeach asked survey participants to priorities which human values were most important to them. Rokeach compiled his findings with a view to developing a homogenised and prioritised set of human values. However, Rokeach found cultural and sub-cultural differences can play a role in the results.

Though there have been numerous researchers before and since Rokeach, arguably his work was most in-depth in terms of methodology and findings. Despite this, Rokeach only made nominal mentions of value dissonance; the lack of alignment between a person's value priorities, and the mismatching value priorities of another. A small amount of research since has shed little light on the subject to allow us to understand the term "offensive" any better.

Thus we can't find the answer to what is considered offensive in law, or a one-size-fits-all rule in societies. Despite this, as individuals living our lives in our own society and subcultures (which often have more specific unspoken rules) we exist, and we mostly do so without offending others in our society.

The offensive act that led to the crisis was the result of thinking (or possibly not taking the time to think enough). It is good practice to try to think differently on complicated and/or sensitive subjects; particularly ones that go against your own values. However not everything is black and white and not everything is as it appears. The next section provides some different perspectives on crisis issues and helps to pave the way to thinking differently. Following these suggestions increases your ability to out-think a crisis, facilitates working with stakeholders, and aids in leading an organisation to being the best in its industry.

6.1.1 Acknowledge That the Act Is Considered Offensive

If the situation is already a crisis, then stakeholders are already offended, and the news media has taken an interest in the crisis stakeholder's viewpoints. Unless you want to be seen as bickering about how people feel, which is internal to them and has no place for accommodating your organisation, then it is best to accept that they feel the way they do, and acknowledge that they feel offended.

To debate on whether or not people should be offended is well beyond the realm of dealing with a reputational crisis. If someone is offended, then they have had an emotional response to what they perceive as an offensive act. Thus to debate if someone should be offended makes it seem as though you think you are not only a moral authority but also their personal psychologist and psychiatrist and somehow qualified to discuss their emotional reactions to certain things.

6.1.2 Association with the Offensive Act

Some crisis communication literature engages with the historical behaviour of an organisation. That is, if a company has a history of offensive acts, then it is more likely that the crisis will be more intense, for a longer period, and will have greater negative impacts on the company. However, as is often the case that the company does not have a history of offensive acts and reputational crises, then it may be possible to distance the offensive act from the company. That is to say, the single offensive act is an anomaly in the company's behaviour, and does not represent how the company normally operates. In this case it may be possible to situate the offensive act outside the company's reputation. Another way of viewing this is to say that the stakeholders are upset with the offensive act, but not perse with the company (which has a history of good behaviour). This method is however limited in its application, for if the offensive act is too extreme and at foresight would have been an avoidable offensive act, then the offensive act may not be forgiven as it is not really a misstep, rather a calculated risk.[1]

6.1.3 *Why and How to Apologise*

In part crisis communication literature and research is solely focussed on avoiding apologising and taking responsibility, for fear of "weakening its legal position in the event of a lawsuit" (Coombs & Holladay, 2002, p. 166). To a very limited degree, not apologising helps avoid liability issues. However a lack of contrition is more likely to fuel anger amongst upset stakeholders, and quickly lead to lawsuits. Unless you want to come across as arrogant, and out of touch, and out of reach then first you have to acknowledge that stakeholders are offended. Regardless if you think they are right or wrong in being offended, their feelings are personal and not for you to judge. Next it might be decent to apologise for causing the stakeholders offense. That still doesn't mean you have committed an offending act. Instead it means that you have empathy for them feeling offended. For example, you might express empathy for someone losing a loved one by saying you are sorry for their loss. That does not make you the killer of their loved one. It shows that you are sorry that they are feeling that way. Similarly you can feel sorry that someone is offended, without carrying the blame for the offending act.

[1]For a more personal example; if one of your friends accidentally ran over one of your pets, you could probably manage forgiveness. In the first instance you would attribute the offensiveness of killing the pet to an accident, or situational, but you would not immediately decide your friend is a pet killer. But if your friend did it a number of times, you would certainly question the situation and your friend's moral compass. The intent of the offensive act also matters significantly. For example, if your pet annoyed your friend, and your friend made her dislike of the pet obvious, and then ran over your pet, you would likely make a character judgement of your friend almost immediately.

6.1.4 *Is It a Crisis? Are the Crisis and the Target of a Crisis Not the Same Thing?*

An offensive act in a crisis is not the same as the organisation. The offensive act only represents the offensive act itself, and the associated outcomes of the offensive act. In some crises the associated outcomes of an offensive act might be fatalities or injuries. Regardless of your viewpoint of the organisation (if you are CEO or a protestor), neither fatalities nor injuries are in the least bit desirable. Another example might be a crisis where the offensive act is fraud, in which case you might be able to empathise with it personally by thinking ‘I would not be pleased if my accountant defrauded me’. The purpose of these examples is to explain that news media and stakeholders take issue with the offensive act, but do not necessarily relate them to the organisation’s typical behaviour until the organisation (a) accepts ownership of the offensive act, and (b) tries to justify the offensive act.

If instead the organisation (a) accepts ownership of the offensive act, and (b) denounces the offensive act, then the organisation may quickly be able to resolve the crisis with communicating empathy, apology, and corrective action. In such an instance, the offensive act is denounced as not being within the company’s ethical ideals and the stakeholders can work together with the company to resolve the adverse impacts and develop a best practice strategy to prevent future occurrences of the same across the industry.

For example, a company that conducts ethical reviews for other companies might make a blunder and be held to account for an ethically unsound decision. Normally this could be devastating for the company as the offending act is directly related to its daily operation. But if the company denounces the ethically unsound decision, and takes a pro-active approach and through the process develops new and improved best practice methods, the company could instead improve its reputation for ethical reasoning, decision making, and developing a highly regarded ethical framework.

In summary; the subject of a crisis can be the offensive act, whilst the target of the crisis does not necessarily have to be the company. Instead the target can be operational standards and practices. This strategy allows for the company to invite stakeholders to engage with a process to develop better practices and thereby resolve the current crisis and prevent future crises of the same nature.

6.2 Viewing Preventative Measures Differently

Since stakeholders are offended by an act, and it is not up to anyone else to say that someone should not be offended, the situation has reached crisis point, and without any imagination it is easy to see that a repeat of the offending act in a similar context will cause stakeholders to be offended again. Since no one wants a reputational crisis, it is reasonable to think that you want to avoid the same situation, thus it makes sense to say “I will make sure this won’t happen again”. If the offending act is part of the day to day operations of an organisation then how that act is perceived should be reviewed, but not in the midst of a crisis. In other words, find a different way to contextualise the act, but do it at a time when there is no crisis. Frame the act within an acceptable standard of social responsibility. For further information on corporate social responsibility, a good place to start is ISO 26000 by the International Standards Association (International Organisation for Standarization, 2020).

Enacting preventative measures basically means that you won't be doing the same thing in future, if you can help it at all. If you do exactly the same thing, it will lead to the same result; a reputational crisis. Please see Chap. 8 of this book which is dedicated to preventative measures.

6.3 Making Reparations

Making reparations and compensation generally go hand in hand. Both these actions mean to make good and reset the game so that everyone has been dealt with in a fair way. In some crises, company CEO's hid behind the veils of their legal team and cower when faced with financial reparations and compensation. However in many crises, the offending act was the result of (a mishap during) day to day operations, which required the stakeholders to contribute to the operations to produce the end result the organisation sought. Thus the stakeholders are an intrinsic part of the operations, and if those operations have caused an occasion of suffering or harm to the contributing stakeholders, it is reasonable to suggest that the stakeholders are owed their dues. Though this is a crude way of putting it, the stakeholders being affected was negative side effect of doing business, and thus it may be reasonable that they be compensated.

Typically it goes against the focus of the company (which is to create a maximum return for its shareholders) to give monies to stakeholders. However if the stakeholder's situation is being adversely affected due to the normal operations of a company, then likely a court will hold the company to account for adequately compensating those stakeholders. When it is foreseeable that a court would make such a ruling, it is advisable to be proactive in this situation and offer stakeholders a form of compensation. It is likely that not all stakeholders would agree that the amount of compensation offered is adequate and some might still seek more compensation through appealing to a court. Should such an appeal be successful, the other affected stakeholders would seek equal compensation through the courts. Often such large and sudden demand upon the company's financial resources will have an instant downward effect the company's share price. The most effective means to mitigate the sudden (and shocking) drop in company share price may be to pre-empt the impact by offering a reasonable amount of compensation. This way the company share price will make the adjustment prior to any law suits and any resulting ruling will often be favourable to the company. Last but not least, it is fair to compensate stakeholders for their losses that have occurred as a result of arguably unethical practices.

6.4 Summary of Crisis Management Challenges

Without doubt, there are many challenges in existing crisis communication and management theory and practice. It is presumptive to believe that everything is being done as well as it could be done, particularly if we look to the recent reputational crises of some of the most well-resourced companies in the world (many of these companies are worth more than the Gross Domestic Product of half a dozen nations). In reputational crises, often the lives of many stakeholders are affected, both inside and outside the organisation experiencing the crisis. The existing models to deal with crises do not offer enough to deal with the stakeholders and some models take stakeholders for granted as a petty nuisance that should only be understood for the sole purpose of solving a crisis so the organisation can go back to its normal operations. This critical review of the research and practice likely will not be well received by the respective communities that are researchers and practitioners. But there is no holy grail if we are to be sincere about continues improvements and have the humility to recognise there is always room for improvement. Academics will take issue with this review because in a sense it undermines a lot of the assumptions on which a lot of their research is based and generally goes against the grain of the (conservative) thinking. For example, resituating stakeholders in a crisis would be considered problematic (but ironically not likely by the designer of contemporary stakeholder theory). Practitioners in crisis communication, whether they be in-house staff of larger companies or consultants, are likely to take issue with the notion that their current tool kit for dealing with crises is incomplete, and likely has to be reconfigured. However it is not enough to stick with the current practices in research and application in the field just because it is heavily relied upon. If that were a reasonable and accepted way of thinking, this would be written on stone tablets in hieroglyphics.

The following chapters outline some key principles in improving the way we deal with reputational crises and provide some examples of how these may be applied.

6.5 Fluidity in Dealing with Crises and Conflicting Stakeholder Interests

The existing literature on crisis communication is largely centred on which messages to deliver when, to whom, and how. Another point of view on dealing with crises may be helpful to understand how to deal with crises that do not fit the typical patterns or scenarios that are often studied. To do this, it is helpful to understand the concept of fluidity in crises, crisis stakeholders, and the media.

Central to a crisis are the crisis stakeholders. For without crisis stakeholders, there is no crisis. This means it is important to communicate with salient crisis stakeholders and get the messages and priorities right the first time whenever possible.

6.5.1 Stakeholder Viewpoints

The vast majority of this book is centred on the concept of a crisis happening at the time. However, good planning and due diligence in corporate governance means that companies should be testing their messages with various stakeholders, in case the messages cause a crisis, or simply just to test the suitability of the messages for when a crisis does occur.

There are numerous methods currently being employed by organisations to engage with stakeholders. Be it for community forums to discuss town planning, citizen of the year, user participations surveys, telephone surveys at the end of a service call, and many more.

A quick glimpse at all of these strategies nearly always gives the impression that the stakeholder/community member is there to serve as a stakeholder to the organisation. Online forms for the citizen of the year are a perfect example. In this, a local government organisation was seeking nominees for the prestigious honour of being named citizen of the year. Unfortunately though, the local government had outsourced the web based nomination process through a company which is operated from the other side of the world, and the questions look more like a security services interrogation of personal details for both the nominee and the nominator. The nominator is assumed to be so personally familiar with the nominee that he/she is expected to know the nominee's date of birth, address, and phone number. This example shows how much the local government is only looking at the situation from their own perspective. Whereas in a more stakeholder centred strategy, the local government would only maybe outsource the project, and if so, to a local company, and it would not be seeking to get all those personal details from any party. Instead it would simply ask for a unique identifying data for both parties to ensure that it cannot be defrauded.

If we transpose this concept to crisis communications, we would then start to look at how we gather information and engage with our stakeholders very differently. For instance, in crisis preparation an organisation would seek to engage with its genuine stakeholders and find out what is important to them. The idea would then be to find out what would be most concerning to the stakeholders, and subsequently ask the stakeholders what would be considered satisfactory solutions to those concerns. This would provide a very useful guide on likely stakeholder responses during and after a crisis, forming a tentative plan for mapping stakeholder salience during a reputational crisis.

The very basic fundamentals of a crisis means there is a problem that has to be dealt with. Be it that the problem is caused by external or internal stakeholders, or that the events were controllable or uncontrollable. The problem remains the same, in that it exists for at least some, if not all actors involved. This in turn means that the different viewpoints held by different stakeholders involved in the crisis, are all valid in the context of them being stakeholders. In other words, if the stakeholder has legitimacy as a stakeholder, then the stakeholder's viewpoint of the crisis may also have legitimacy.

For example, when a mining company is seeking to build a materials transport terminal in an environmentally protected coral reef area, the following opposing viewpoints are valid;

- Company "we need this terminal to enable and boost our business operations"
- Local tourism company "we cannot have the mining company's terminal in our reef because it will destroy the beauty and thereby the tourism industry"
- Local politician "we need this terminal for the jobs, but we need it to be nominal so it doesn't significantly affect the natural environment"
- Environmentalist "this reef does not belong to people, and definitely not just to our generation. It belongs to the earth in perpetuity"
- Local resident "we need a safe and clean environment for us and our kids, and we need jobs"
- Federal politician "we need this project to increase our exports and create jobs"

All these viewpoints are valid and each of them held by legitimate stakeholders. The legitimacy of these stakeholders is evident in that they are affected and/or can affect the project. Some of the stakeholders have urgency and/or power. But all of them are legitimate, which means that we have to take them into account when developing a solution. The best solution would be to take into account all of the stakeholder's viewpoints, and develop a model that suits everyone equally. It would however be impossible to develop a solution that serves everyone completely. Thus finding acceptable compromises amongst all stakeholders would realise the solution. This example serves well to illustrate that a company experiencing a crisis might not initially want to negotiate with what are arguably opponents to its operations. However some negotiations to find an acceptable middle ground will often provide a reasonable and reasoned solution to both the company and its stakeholders.

6.5.2 Blame

As a rule reputational crises are blame focussed. Through our lives we understand that blame is the attribution of wrong doing. As a child we learn that bad behaviour is punished and good behaviour is rewarded. However as cynical this may be; through our adult life we often learn that some people are guilty of bad behaviour and aren't punished, and that other's good behaviour is never rewarded. Of course this is not how we want society to be, for otherwise we wouldn't even bother having a legal system and instead just let the criminals walk free and carry on with their bad behaviour. Thus it is an almost natural response to punish people or organisations for behaving badly. The legal system's ambition is to correct bad behaviour and (hopefully) shape the imprisoned criminals to be better citizens. Yet this seems to be beyond the ambition of society if we only choose to blame and punish bad behaviour. In an only slightly more sophisticated society, we punish those organisations that do wrong, but we wouldn't leave it at that. We would take that one step further and develop a system for correcting the behaviour of organisations who behaved badly.

In our personal lives, we often find it easy to blame our spouse for not understanding us, our children for testing our patience, and our colleagues for making errors. Yet blame alone does little more than to make the others feel bad, and redeem ourselves of any wrong doing. That is not to say that the person held to account for bad behaviour is completely innocent of that claim. But if we take the opportunity to understand why our spouse does not understand us, or why our children are at times demanding, we would nearly always find that there is something we can do, to remedy the cause of the problem. And naturally our relationships improve as a result. Discussions such as those are nearly impossible to hold if there is no respect, or no aim to build or rebuild trust. The most disarming way to initiate those discussions is by taking blame out of the equation and focussing on what caused things to go wrong; "What was lacking and how can we fix this?" Often the reason we don't pursue this method of diffusing a situation is because generally people are offended by the accusation of bad behaviour and, like most traditional crisis communication strategies, people try their hardest to defend their actions in one of many ways. But they are mostly only defending their actions as a means of defending their egos, or protecting their image. Oftentimes people can see how their actions were seen to be bad from your perspective, but they are unwilling to admit total responsibility, or they are so busy defending themselves that they haven't given any more thought on how the behaviour was seen as bad behaviour or that the action may have been wrong.

This strategy nearly always works in our personal lives, yet in society and the media it is rarely heard about. Perhaps in our personal lives, some of us have the emotional intelligence to look beyond a dispute or argument whilst it is happening. When we do that, we can differentiate between the offending act and ourselves. This means of distancing ourselves from the offending act and the resulting argument allows us to work together with the other party to seek a resolution. To use this strategy in crisis communications, we must look at how we have used stakeholder theory in crisis communications, and how we can use it differently.

6.6 Developing New Stakeholder Maps

Contemporary reputational crisis communication strategies are in part based on the traditional stakeholder theory whereby the company is situated at the centre of the stakeholder map and stakeholders on the periphery. However, reputational crises can be solved using a different approach; using an adaptation of Freeman's later stakeholder theory modelling.

While still using some of the design principles of the traditional stakeholder theory, but removing a few of the boundaries that come with it, allows the stakeholder map to have the crisis placed at the centre. Arguably a crisis on its own is not a stakeholder, and should therefore not be part of a stakeholder map. However a crisis is nothing if it does not have stakeholders. When we place the crisis at the centre of the map, it allows us to show a more unbiased stakeholder map of the crisis that aids in developing a solution to the crisis.

Placing the crisis at the centre of the stakeholder map allows us to have a less biased perspective of the crisis in terms of who really is involved in the crisis. That is to say, who is affected by the crisis, and who can affect the crisis. This strategy allows the focus to be on the crisis itself, who the crisis affects, and who can affect the crisis.

Example – Jeremy Clarkson Reputational Crisis
Situation:

As one of three hosts of the very popular television show Top Gear, Jeremy Clarkson enjoyed somewhat of celebrity status and thus anything he did was considered newsworthy. It was rumoured that Clarkson had an excitable temper which was fuelled by him drinking more than what was healthy. During a more heated moment of Clarkson's excitable temper a physical altercation occurred between Clarkson and one member of the show's production team. When it became a news story and rose to prominence in the mainstream media, the production company, BBC, decided enough was enough and the show was cancelled as it was held the BBC's reputation would not be associated with the antics.

Stakeholder map – Traditional strategy

Using the traditional model of stakeholder theory to map out this situation crisis places Clarkson at the centre, or the BBC at the centre (depending on which organisation is being represented) (Fig. 6.1).

Stakeholder map – thinking differently

In this example, the crisis itself is at the centre, with Clarkson, the BBC, the audience, BBC staff, sponsors, all affected by the crisis. An extrapolation of this

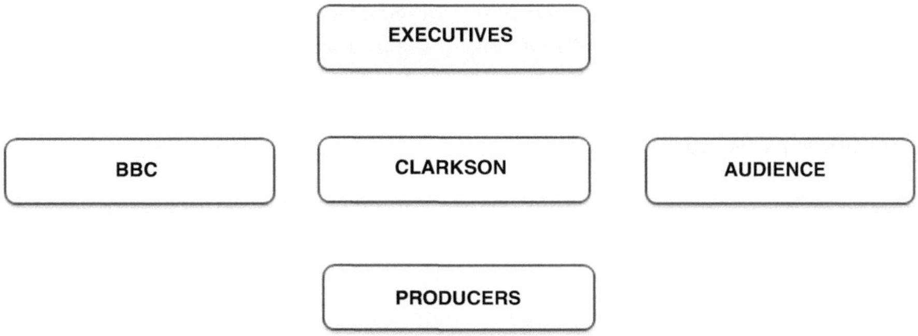

Fig. 6.1 Traditional stakeholder viewpoint – Jeremy Clarkson

Fig. 6.2 Thinking differently on stakeholder viewpoint – Jeremy Clarkson

would include alcohol beverage association Alcoholics Anonymous (as the crisis issue is in part the reason their organisation exists) (Fig. 6.2).

New crisis outcome

Focussing on the crisis itself makes it easier for the issue to be resolved to mutual satisfaction of all crisis stakeholders. In reality BBC discontinued the very profitable Top Gear show, which was immediately picked up as a lucrative deal for another television company. The actual problem was not solved at all.

Instead if the crisis itself was at the centre of the stakeholder map, it would have changed the dynamics for the stakeholders and how they all dealt with the situation. For example, Alcoholics Anonymous (AA) could have called on the BBC and Clarkson to discuss a way out of the situation, as AA would have been a stakeholder to the crisis. BBC and AA could have worked with Clarkson on how alcohol affects behaviours, and for example, at the end of each episode, Clarkson could have given a weekly account for how he is dealing with changing his alcohol consumption. This would have engaged his audience (also stakeholders) with those ideas and possibly ideals. Clarkson could have used his prominent position to advocate to his audience that alcohol abuse isn't great for anyone. This would have made Clarkson a reformed hero, the BBC executives well paid, the audience kept honestly informed, AA with a strong supporter, and alcoholics with a narrative by their idol on how to end alcohol addiction.

Example – BP Reputational Crisis
Situation:

BP (British Petroleum) owned an off shore oil platform operation in the Gulf of Mexico when it sprang a leak, killing staff, and spilling oil into the Gulf.

Stakeholder map – Traditional strategy

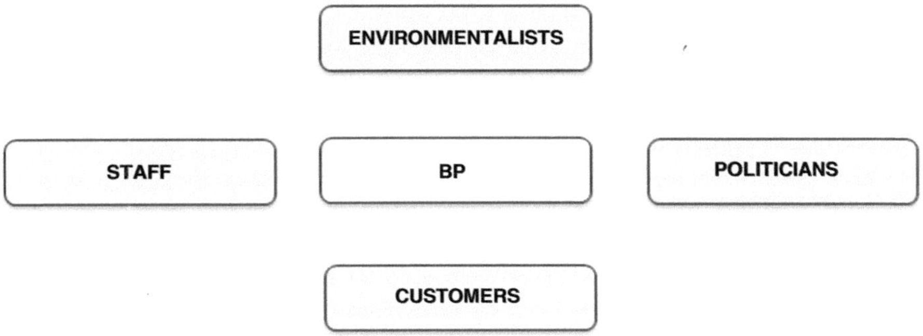

Fig. 6.3 Traditional stakeholder viewpoint – BP

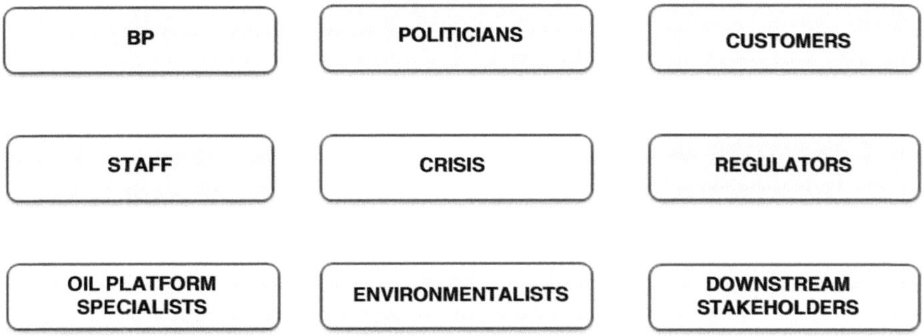

Fig. 6.4 Thinking differently on stakeholder viewpoint – BP

BP is placed at the centre of the stakeholder map and staff, customers, environmentalists and politicians are plàce on the periphery (Fig. 6.3).

Stakeholder map – thinking differently

Using a crisis centred approach to the problem BP would instead be placed on the periphery together with all other crisis stakeholders with who BP would have to work to solve the crisis (Fig. 6.4).

New crisis outcome

Using this approach, it is very clear that the company has to work with regulators, environmentalists, politicians, and oil platform specialists, to name but a few. BP could have focussed on a solution that worked equitably for most stakeholders, and facilitated an open invitation for global experts in leaks for oil platforms to assist in the recovery. It also makes it easier for the company to extrapolate the existing (downstream) stakeholder maps for environmental impacts to include potential claimants such as fishermen and real estate agencies. Working together with these newly discovered crisis stakeholders allows many options and possible salient stakeholders to be revealed.

This would have resulted in BP having a more pro-active approach to fines, penalties and compensation, allowing the stock market to calculate a more precise market impact instead of negative speculation. For solving the problem itself, all stakeholders affected would have been supportive of BP seeking a solution with stakeholders as opposed to being focussed on blaming BP. For instance, numerous global experts from all fields could have immediately worked together to develop a quick solution to stop the leak. Similarly, the subsequently better informed fishing operators would have been able to forecast the impact of the spill, and mitigated their financial impacts to some extent. When more prepared for the situation environmentalists would have been able to enact strategies to safeguard wildlife whilst the spill containment was being developed and implemented.

Example – Dreamworld Reputational Crisis
Situation:

The Gold Coast theme park, Dreamworld, had been in operation for decades with many exciting rides for young and old. When during one of the many rides a vessel holding passengers turned and stayed upside down, and drowned those passengers. Initially the theme park made a statement which suggested it would close for a few days. However during subsequent media updates, the company continuously extended the date for reopening, which led to many press releases contradicting many formerly given reopening dates. The company cited safety checks for reasons for the delays.

Naturally, as rides are a large part of the theme park's day to day operations, this caused a significant reputational crisis.

Stakeholder map – Traditional strategy

The traditional stakeholder map would have included the affected passengers (victims), and their families. In addition to the theme park itself at the centre of the crisis stakeholder map, the overseeing legislative bodies, staff, and so forth would also have featured (Fig. 6.5).

Fig. 6.5 Traditional stakeholder viewpoint – Dreamworld

Fig. 6.6 Thinking differently on stakeholder viewpoint – Dreamworld

Stakeholder map – thinking differently

Placing the crisis at the centre of the crisis stakeholder map would have made it easier for Dreamworld to include other stakeholders in its thinking, and see the crisis more easily from different stakeholders' perspectives. In doing so, Dreamworld would possibly have given more focus on how legislators and potential future customers would view the company and its operations (there is no point re-opening a theme park to potential customers so they can go on rides risking their lives) (Fig. 6.6).

New crisis outcome

Dreamworld would have been viewed to consider the risks and importance of their customer's safety more important if they had taken a crisis centred approach to solving the issue. It would have been more productive, and more decent to close the theme park for several weeks and issue a statement to that effect. This would at least have developed the notion that it takes its customer's safety seriously.

Also using a crisis centred stakeholder map, the company likely would have reasoned that despite the terrible event, the company was well placed to make itself the safest theme park in operation. They could have taken the control of the situation by asking for leading safety experts to consult on a panel to develop a world's best practice safety standards. This would have kept the customers safe, indicated remorse, improved the company's reputation, given guidance to their shareholders, and compelled other theme parks to increase their safety standards.

Summary

The focus of reputations crisis communications strategies is often defending the reputation, and often also defending the offensive act. Yet it is counterintuitive to place the organisation at the centre of that stakeholder map, as the loss of lives and potential loss of lives of future customers would have to be of paramount importance. These examples show that an organisation experiencing a reputational crisis should be focussed on fixing the issue itself, rather than simply trying to appease stakeholders with the focus being reputational integrity. Particularly, as the reputational integrity is in a state of flux during a reputational crisis.

6.7 Implied Rules of Conduct

Neither cultural studies nor studies of human values can help us understand the notion of 'offensive'. For the purposes of expediency, it may be more useful to understand what constitutes good behaviour by an organisation, then what constitutes bad behaviour by an organisation.

6.7.1 Corporate Social Responsibility

Although the original conception of stakeholder theory by Freeman is not perfect for solving reputational crises, it did assist with the development of corporate social responsibility research and practice. Freeman (2004, p. 229) noted

> When the main academic audience for my ideas became people who taught business and society or corporate social responsibility or business ethics I was surprised.

Though the idea of corporate social responsibility has been around for a long time (Dodd, 1932), there has been a larger volume of research into corporate social responsibility since Freeman's (1984) stakeholder theory, and it has found a substantial role in corporate governance. More recently, triple bottom line reporting has been added to the philosophies of corporate governance. Triple bottom line reporting refers to companies not only reporting on financial, but also reporting on social and environmental goals, achievements, and outcomes.

Organisations experience a crisis when they are held to account for an offending act. In other words, the organisation is being held to account for doing the wrong thing. Corporate social responsibility provides a platform doing the right thing.

The International Organisation for Standardization (I.S.O) developed ISO 26000, as an international standard for Corporate Social Responsibility (CSR). The standard is a voluntary measure for companies and organisations to adopt with the view to being corporate better citizens. ISO 26000 cites "two fundamental practices of social responsibility" as "recognising social responsibility" and "stakeholder identification and engagement" (International Organisation for Standarization, 2020).

Suggesting a holistic approach and interdependence, ISO 26000 lists seven core subjects in corporate social responsibility (International Organisation for Standarization, 2020). These being;

- Organisational governance
- Human rights

- Labour practices
- The environment
- Fair operating practices
- Consumer issues
- Community involvement and development

In addition, ISO 26000 lists the principles of CSR to be; "accountability, transparency, ethical behaviour, respect for stakeholder interests, respect for the rule of law, respect for international norms of behaviour, and respect for human rights" (International Organisation for Standarization, 2020).

These principles and core subjects inform organisations to develop a more collaborative approach to *how* organisations operate within their environments, and that their operation's philosophy is more in line with symbiotic relationships in their environments. That is to say; the role organisations take in their environments should include being focussed on what is good for their environments, as what is good for the organisation's environment is generally good for the organisation ('s growth) as well. This is supported with some of Key's (1999) critique of Freeman's original (1984) stakeholder theory being company centric, which is not conducive to growing the operating environment of the company.

Since the 1980's there has been an ever increasing volume of research on corporate social responsibility, closely followed by an increase in corporate social responsibility practices being taken up by organisations. Today there are many standards for corporate social responsibility, and arguably ISO 26000 by the International Organisations for Standardization is one of the most extensive and well renowned. As many new ideas and concepts, it is a work in progress and will evolve as circumstances change. ISO 26000 provides a balanced insight into a more comprehensive engagement of stakeholders, taking into account the welfare of various stakeholder types, and the sustainability of stakeholders in the organisation's operating environment. Hence in terms of how to deal with stakeholders in reputational crises, corporate social responsibility provides a reasonable synopsis of what good organisational conduct looks like, and how it should fit into society without being offensive.

In other words, to solve a reputational crisis we need to exercise good conduct. Although a vast amount of research on reputational crises suggests that the way out of a crisis it to say the right thing for the right situation, the solution may nearly always be found in good conduct and communicating that effectively to salient stakeholders and the media. To instead focus on an excuse for the offensive conduct oftentimes is counterproductive to solving the crisis, as demonstrated by Benoit & Drew's research (Benoit & Drew, 1997). Instead of focussing on blame to deal with crisis, it is better to focus on solutions and preventative strategies.

Bibliography

Benoit, W. L. (1997). Image repair discourse and crisis communication. *Public Relations Review, 23*, 177–186.

Benoit, W. L., & Drew, S. (1997). Appropriatness and effectiveness of image repair strategies. *Communication Reports, 10*, 153–163.

Coombs, W. T., & Holladay, S. J. (2002). Helping crisis managers protect reputational assets – Initial tests of the situational crisis communication theory. *Management Communication Quarterly, 16*(2), 165–186.

Dodd, E. M. (1932). For whom are coporate managers trustees? *Harvard Law Review, XLV*(7), 1145–1163.

Freeman, R. E. (1984). *Strategic management: A stakeholder approach*. Marschfield: Pitman Publishing Inc.

Freeman, R. E. (2004). The stakeholder approach revisited. *Zeitschrift fur Wirtschaft – un Unternnehmensethik, 5*(3), 228–241.

International Organisation for Standarization. (2020). *Schematic overview of ISO 26000*. Retrieved March 2020, from International Organisation for Standarization. https://www.iso.org/publication/PUB100260.html

Jandt, F. E. (2010). *An introduction to intercultural communication*. Thousand Oaks: Sage.

Key, S. (1999). Toward a new theory of the firm: A critique of stakeholder "theory". *Management Decision, 37*(4), 317–328.

Rokeach, M. (1973). *The nature of human values*. New York: Free Press.

Stefanova, M. (2001, January). The price of tourism: Land alienation in Vanuatu. *World Bank – Justice for the Poor, 2*(1), 1.

Chapter 7
Best Practice Method of Dealing with Reputational Crises

Abstract Resituating the company on a stakeholder map and replacing the focus to be on the crisis itself, rather than just the company permits all actors to work together towards a commonly shared goal; ending the reputational crisis, and preventing future crisis events.

Once we move the focus to solving the crisis, we can be more effective and sincere when using apologia. We can also be more precise in determining how the stakeholders were affected without the distraction of blame, as the focus moves to resolution and prevention. In other words, we can more precisely determine what the cause was, instead of focussing on who caused it. We can then also move onto making reparations and developing preventative strategies as the focus has shifted from blame to working with stakeholders to prevent future crises.

This chapter includes practical guides and a ten step crisis resolution strategy all which serve to show the improvements that can be made as a result of resituating stakeholders. This chapter is completed with notations regarding possible challenges resultant of this strategy.

This chapter embraces the idea of solving reputational crises effectively using the more useful conceptualisation of stakeholder theory. The theoretical backdrop provided in previous chapters gives credence to enacting effective crisis communication and crisis management strategies that engage with the issues at the centre of the reputational crisis with the help of the salient crisis stakeholders. Next, the practical elements of using this strategy to solve reputational crises are proposed and their functionalities are discussed. Following this, the effective theories, practices, and resituated stakeholder theory are summarised into a detailed ten step instruction to solving reputational crises, including media statement templates that engage with the more proactive and considered stakeholder theory. This chapter is completed with a section discussing concerns and limitations of this crisis communication theory.

The crises examples used thus far exemplify the need for a better way of dealing not just with crises, but also how we view stakeholders. If, for instance we dealt with

T. Schermer, *Reputational Crises Unspun*, https://doi.org/10.1007/978-981-16-5130-4_7

crises in a more effective manner, each crisis should hypothetically be the launch pad for the organisation to do things better. We should use crises to improve operational outcomes to better meet the needs of the overall environment, and each crisis would quickly turn from being a large problem, to being a positive and promotional opportunity for the organisation to show how it puts its best foot forward.

It should be suffice to say that the founder of contemporary stakeholder theory himself, Edward Freeman, has had concerns about the use his first version of stakeholder theory. Stakeholder theory was beneficial through furthering research and thinking about stakeholders in that it gave a necessary boost to the earlier forms of corporate social responsibility, and creating the need for triple bottom line reporting. Schools of thought on stakeholder theory have evolved for decades, albeit slowly and stubbornly. Hence seems counterintuitive to still employ the original and oversimplified concept as the centrepiece for solving reputational crises.

In summary, there are too many examples of stakeholders being dealt within wrongly, or in an inappropriate manner. When the foundations for contemporary crisis communication theory and best practice are based on the fundamental principle of organisational centric stakeholder theory, it seems inevitable that crisis communications will often fail to appease stakeholders and the environment in which the crisis occurs.

7.1 Solving a Reputational Crisis

The remainder of this Chapter is focussed on the practical aspects of solving reputational crises, starting with a flow chart on how to solve a crisis, followed with personnel requirements, and how to deal with stakeholders (including the media) during the crisis, and press release templates. Not all strategies and tasks are suitable for every crisis situation. However the generic frameworks set out should be sufficient for an organisation to fill in the specific details and make nominal adjustments. In various circumstances some additional resource allocation may be required.

There are many options available during the course of a reputational crisis, particularly at the beginning of the crisis. The following diagram (see Fig. 7.1 below) illustrates the different pathways that typically present themselves during the initial stages of a reputational crisis.

In the above flowchart all but one specific path lead to an escalation in the crisis. Although crises may not always exactly follow this path, it gives a good indication of the different junctions at which a crisis can turn for the worse through further offending stakeholders. Also note, that not every occasion of the crises escalating means that the crisis can or cannot be solved. Each crisis has its own unique set of circumstances and stakeholder circumstances. However in trying to ensure that the organisation has the best chance of resolving the crises in the shortest period of time, the above pathway is a useful tool.

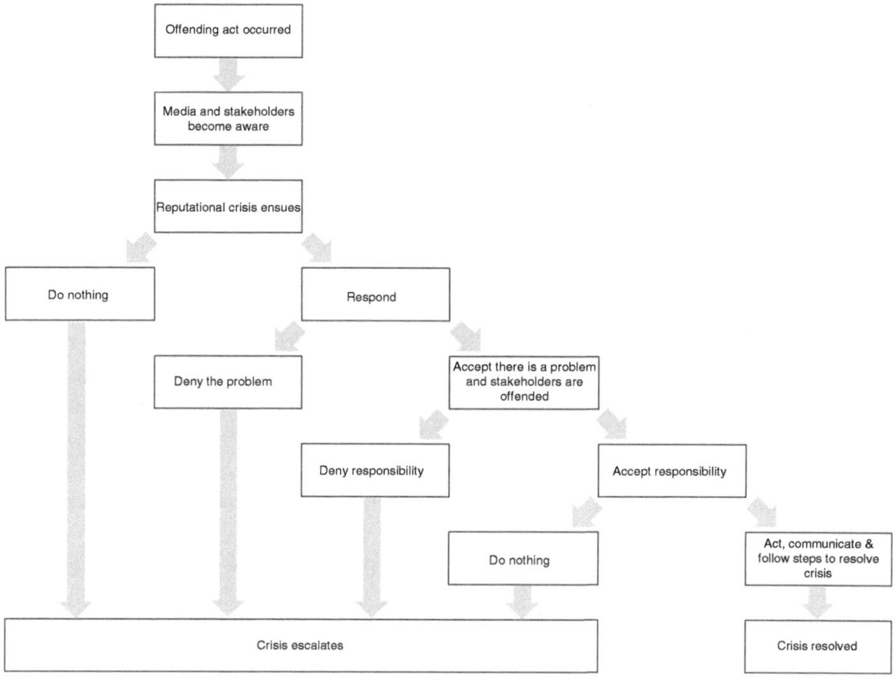

Fig. 7.1 Crisis pathways flowchart

The fundamental principle of the above pathway to solving a crisis is to take ownership of the situation and improve the situation for stakeholders and the organisation. This means accepting that stakeholders are offended, thus not debating that they should or should not feel offended. It does not necessarily demand that the organisation take the blame for the offending act but it does empower the organisation to take proactive steps to limiting and reducing crisis impacts on stakeholders and the organisation.

The remainder of this chapter is devoted to solving reputational crises and engaging stakeholders of the crisis to help solve the crisis. The first section discusses crisis panels in some detail laying the foundation for the next sections detailing a ten step strategy to resolving reputational crises.

7.2 Crisis Panels

What is a crisis panel? A crisis panel is a collective of stakeholders, including representative/s from the organisation, which discusses proposed crisis messages and crisis strategies, in a confidential but egalitarian setting with the aim of solving the crisis to mutual satisfaction.

7.2.1 Purpose

The objective is to develop crises outcomes that have the least negative impact on stakeholders and the organisation (and resolve the crisis as soon as possible) whilst embracing the opportunity to develop a best practice model or method to stop these events happening again in the future, both in the organisation and in the industry.

Because the aim of the panel is to focus on developing a solution to the crisis, instead of attributing blame or cause to a single group, stakeholder, or the organisation, the panel should be egalitarian to facilitate unrestricted responses from aggrieved and offended stakeholders. It serves the organisation experiencing the crisis best if stakeholder responses can be anticipated through this panel, to enable the panel to adequately deal with stakeholder objections prior to media statements or other stakeholder communications. In short, it makes sense to use panels to address concerns before they are in the public domain.

Although at times, panels may appear to go too far in a direction that only serves the organisation's stakeholders, these directions may lead to discoveries on what the best practice or standard could be in an industry. Instead of seeing this as an obstacle, it should be seen as an opportunity to lead the industry with stakeholder support. Organisations can use this information to be proactive and thereby pre-empting potential legislative changes that would further challenge their operations.

Successful Crisis Panel Outcomes

A successful crisis panel outcome would be one where:

- All stakeholders have been respected, their concerns have been heard, and most of the stakeholder's concerns have been addressed satisfactorily.
- Future crises of the same nature will be avoided
- Future precursors leading to the offending action that caused the crisis are redesigned or monitored perpetually, or both
- All claims, financially or otherwise, have been agreed on in principle. Precise details may be determined immediately at a later date.
- The main strategy and messages for media distribution have been agreed to by the majority of the panel members.

Crisis Panels outside of Crisis

Before and after crisis events, crisis panels can aid in:

(a) Crisis prevention
(b) Improved stakeholder relationships
(c) Increased returns for stakeholders and organisations when not in crisis (and during crises).

It is prudent to develop a crisis panel before a crisis occurs. Typically organisational management is likely to engage with these stakeholder representatives as normal practice on a regular basis. However outside of a crisis, these stakeholder representatives would not normally meet together.

Good crisis planning includes having the Board of Directors, or a similar decision making body, give full support to a crisis panel. This is to make sure that decisions made by the crisis panel only require a quick assessment by the Board of Directors during the crisis, when time is critical.

7.2.2 Methodology

Rules

(a) Panel discussions, findings, and outcomes are to remain confidential, except where the panel has agreed to publicize a course of action or communications. The intellectual content remains property of the panel as a whole.

(b) Like a focus group the panel forum is egalitarian. That is to say; each and every panel member has the same amount of power and right to be heard

(c) Without all salient stakeholders present the panel is ineffective and cannot constitute a quorum.

(d) The organisation experiencing the crisis facilitates the panel discussions and decorum. However, where possible it would be most advantageous to appoint a crisis panel facilitator.

Crisis Panel Facilitator

For the purpose of expedience and maintaining direction in crisis panel discussions as well as a level of decorum, a facilitator is recommended to oversee the crisis panel discussions. The facilitator would be tasked with keeping discussions on point, and where necessary breaking deadlocks in discussions through encouraging new approaches to those deadlocks. Ideally, for the purpose of ensuring integrity in the crisis panel, the facilitator would have a neutral point of view in relation to the crisis focus, cause, subject, and stakeholders. That is to say, the facilitator must be able to ensure that all stakeholders are treated fairly and equally and their concerns are heard and taken into account in developing a mutually agreeable solution to the crisis. For example, if the reputational crisis is that of a food producing company which has been held to account for food poisoning claims, then the facilitator would ensure that the proposed action by the company is satisfactory to the persons affected by the food poisoning, the regulatory authorities, employee's union (as employees could be held to account within the company), food processing factory designers, and the financial ramifications on the company's profitability, and ability to implement those proposed actions. In this example it would be likely that the persons affected by the food poisoning would demand the company install the most strict operations and controls to avoid future food poisonings, and the company would also want to avoid similar incidents. However the precautions installed to ensure it doesn't happen again, should not be to such extremes that the company can no longer operate. Instead, the new precautions should be developed to make the company the best in the food production industry in regards to food poisoning prevention, which it could then claim in consumer marketing campaigns. From this point, the regulatory authorities could redesign their requirements to take into account some of the preventative actions the company then installs. As another example, we could look at the passenger aircraft manufacturer, Boeing, which had a reputational crisis with the Boeing Max crashing in two separate incidents. Upon some publically known investigations, it became obvious that some pilots had already complained about a few aspects in the aircraft's design. With a small amount of imagination, it would be conceivable that users of products including planes will often find shortcomings in design. However if Boeing had used a crisis panel to manage the situation, it would have instantly come to light that this plane's design had some unique problems, and it could have prevented the second plane crash. Furthermore, if Boeing had invited its commercial rival, Airbus, to the crisis panel discussions, Airbus likely would have investigated the causes of the crash as a means to gain more market share. However, this would have enabled Boeing to address those causes and concerns, and through the scrutiny of its commercial rival, been able to redesign the problem areas creating a safer passenger plane. In addition, if the legislated authorities had been present at the crisis panel, it would have learned from Airbus's investigations and critique of Boeing, on how to better manage safety protocols including pilot concerns on safety. This example serves to show how the crisis panel facilitator would be in a tumultuous environment with much directed conflict between the different crisis stakeholders, and demonstrates the need for a crisis panel facilitator to manage the various and strong viewpoints and opinions.

Crisis Panel Composition

(a) The panel composition should be representative of all stakeholders/groups that are salient in the crisis. It is both proactive and tactical to have representatives from the following stakeholder groups included in the panel to ensure all salient stakeholders and groups are satisfied with panel outcomes and to avoid conflict outside of the confines of the crisis panel;

- Crisis affected or afflicted persons
- Emergency personnel (if relevant to this crisis)
- Incumbent politician (as these will play a role in the post crisis legislation changes (regardless if you want those changes, there is now a good chance that will happen))
- Legislated authority (for example; workplace health and safety, food safety authority, consumer protection authority)
- Interest groups. They will otherwise rally against you, and your industry to have legislation changed,
- News media (press)
- The organisation experiencing the crisis

(b) To get the best outcome and most out of the panel, each stakeholder group should attend and be represented equally.

(c) The news media is included as a stakeholder as they generally inform the public. It is most effective to have the news media input in terms of how they are likely to synthesise the crisis messages and outcomes.
(d) Grievances, objections, and offended contributions must be heard, for it is these that are most likely to inflame the crisis outside of the panel.

Crisis Panel Outcomes

(a) Panel members, as representatives of stakeholders/stakeholder groups, are responsible for the dissemination of their own message through news media,
(b) The perfect outcome of panel discussions is that all stakeholders, including the organisation, have reached a mutually satisfactory agreement,
(c) During and after the crisis, the panel will work together to develop best practice standards for the industry.

Limitations

Crisis panels are cautioned to refrain from discussing matters which are;

(a) Legally not permissible (such as illegal activities),
(b) Confidential matters,
(c) Likely to significantly risk the organisation's longevity (the argument here is that if the organisation does not exist in the future, it will not be able to develop a best practice standard which can prevent the offensive event from happening again in the future),
(d) In direct contravention of solving the crisis,
(e) Are not likely to be salient to developing a best practice method for the organisation and industry.

Crisis Panel Design

The following diagrams illustrate the type of crisis panels that are effective for crisis preparation, and crisis management. To allow simplified interpretation and use, the diagrams don't include overlaps between the stakeholder representatives although these do often exist in terms of who they represent. The diagrams also do not show relationships between different stakeholder representatives, although these relationships could be very influential in the crisis panel outcomes. This may be problematic in terms of attempting to establish an egalitarian panel, the (often symbiotic) relationships between stakeholder representatives does exist in the world outside the panel, and may play a role in how the outside world will eventually view the panel's outcomes.

In the following schemas the absence of flow arrows is intentional as to not be instructive in how discussions flow. Each panel member should be free to discuss with any one or all panel members.

The following illustration (Fig. 7.2 below) places the Interest Group at the centre of the crisis panel design, focussing the discussions on the Interest Group.

The next illustration (Fig. 7.3 below) places the Media at the centre of the crisis panel design, focussing the discussions on the Media. This would aid in developing various viewpoints on how the media will perceive the crisis situation.

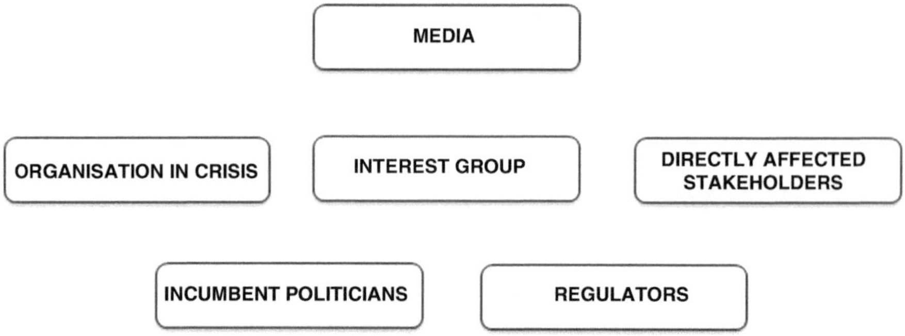

Fig. 7.2 Stakeholder centred: Interest group

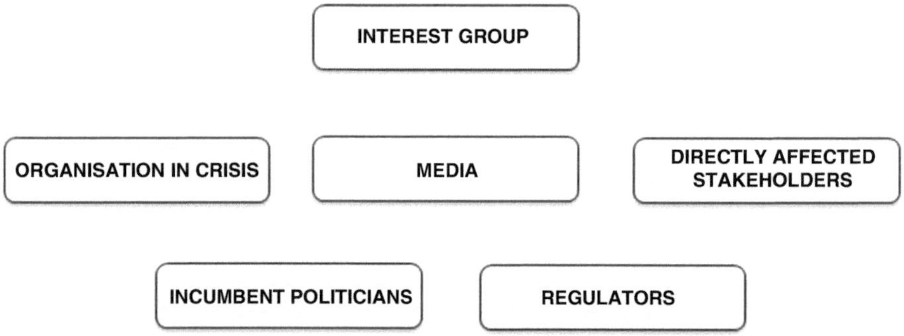

Fig. 7.3 Stakeholder centred: Media

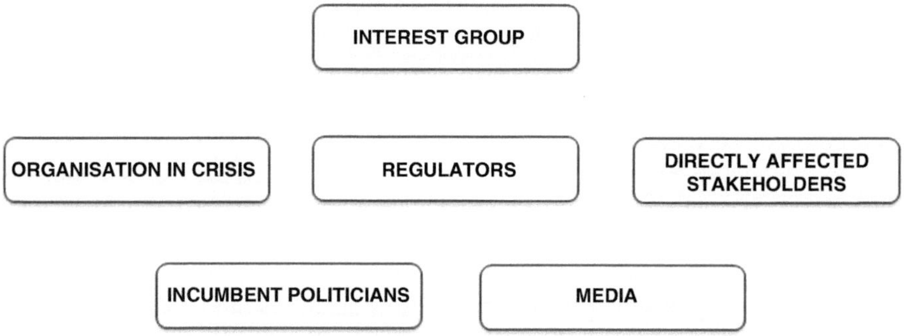

Fig. 7.4 Stakeholder centred: Regulators

The following illustration (Fig. 7.4 above) places the regulators at the centre of the crisis panel design. Discussions held in this crisis panel design will provide significant insights into how the regulators will influence the current crisis, and how future crisis events and operations would be effected if the regulators are able to influence outcomes to their complete satisfaction.

The company centred crisis panel design (see Fig. 7.5 below) is a more typical way of viewing the crisis. Discussions from this panel would likely be company centric, and as often is demonstrated in reputational crises that are covered in mainstream news media, rarely have favourable outcomes for the company.

The crisis panel design below (Fig. 7.6) places the crisis itself at the centre of the panel and allows for all stakeholders to engage with the crisis issue directly, and engage with the crisis issue through other crisis stakeholders.

Concerns About the Non-organisation Centric Panel

Concerns about the removing the organisation in crisis from the centre would be expected from critics. However the organisation is only in crisis for as long as it has stakeholders, of whom the afflicted stakeholders are arguably at the centre of the crisis, together with the organisation. Consequently when stakeholders in a crisis feel they do not get a fair hearing or an equal voice in crisis resolution, the other parties including the media (external to the panel) could give the aggrieved stakeholder a hearing, which by default ensures the crisis will continue. It is for this reason that the focus of a crisis panel is to seek resolution with aggrieved stakeholders through testing messages and strategies for stakeholder responses.

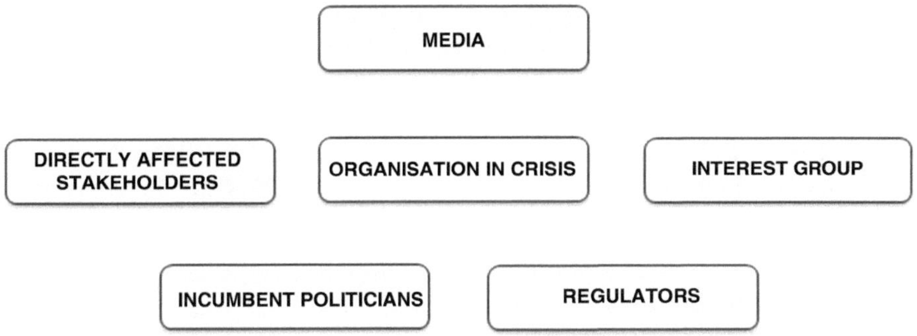

Fig. 7.5 Organisation centred

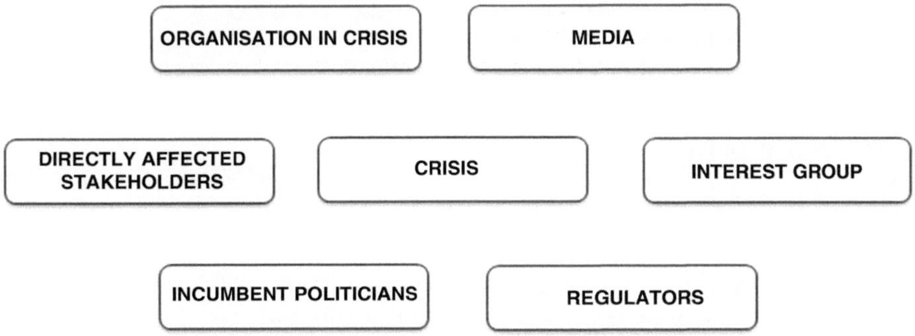

Fig. 7.6 Non-centred crisis panel

The crisis centred panel is proposed as an effective model for successful crisis resolution.

The crisis centred resolution approach allows for:

- the panel to be focussed on the actual crisis, rather than just the organisation
- each member of the panel to have equal contributions;
- solutions not solely focussed on any single specific member;
- each member is enabled to support or not support messages and/or strategies;
- each member of the panel may declare that the crisis resolution is not adequate to facilitate further negotiations. (When a panel member declares dissatisfaction it is an opportunity for the organisation and others to discover a mutually satisfactory solution that will likely end the reputational crisis).

As in any situation where all members have an equal voice, there will be arguments and dissatisfaction. It is the purpose of these panels to deal with claims of dissatisfaction of stakeholders within the confines of the panel, with the objective to satisfying any concerns that may further prolong or exaggerate the crisis.

Crisis panels should be able to develop a way out of the crisis, whereby all stakeholders are mostly satisfied with the outcome, and there has been a contribution to improving the organisation and setting a better standard for the industry. Panel discussion outcomes should be reported in written form, as a single statement (to avoid confusing and technical information) and provide the basis for subsequent media releases, noting how the organisation is moving out of the crisis.

Inconclusive Results from Crisis Panel

In the instance that the panel does not develop a satisfactory solution to the crisis, it will still yield results useful in ending the reputational crisis. As the crisis panel operates somewhat like a focus group, it will have developed a plethora of likely responses from all stakeholders. Those responses will be helpful in drafting:

- Crisis resolution strategies,
- Crisis communication strategies, and
- Crisis communication messages,

Furthermore, should it be the case that the crisis panel does not yield an immediate solution to the crisis, crisis panel discussions and actions will illustrate which stakeholders are supportive, neutral, or opposing to certain strategies. The organisation then has a choice of going forward on it is own preferred strategy, or developing a new crisis panel with stakeholders who are committed to solving the crisis.

Lack of Stakeholder Representation

It would be ideal to form a crisis panel whereby all salient crisis stakeholders are represented. However for any number of reasons it is possible that not all salient stakeholders will be interested in participating in the crisis panel. In such an instance, it would be worthwhile conducting one-on-one discussions with representatives of those salient stakeholders with the objective of getting their viewpoints, opinions, and thoughts and tabling them the at the crisis panel meeting. If some stakeholders can't be represented in the crisis panel for logistical reasons, it may serve them to elect a proxy to speak on their behalf.

Confidentiality in Crisis Panel Discussions
If crisis panel participants feel that their viewpoints may cause conflict in future or directly outside the crisis panel, their contributions will be limited and reduce the effectiveness of the panel. To enable the crisis panel participants to discuss and contribute in the panel most effectively, it is advised that confidentiality agreements are signed by all parties, including members of the organisation experiencing the crisis.

7.3 Appointing a Crisis Communications Manager

Communications with the media and managing crisis communications with stakeholder representatives requires specific skills to make sure the crisis isn't escalated. News media and aggrieved stakeholders may at times attempt to change the focus of proceedings through asking leading questions, or reframing the issue/s, or distracting other's attention to a less salient issue. Therefore it is important to have a skilled communicator managing the public (face) image of the organisation who is able to manage those challenges without distraction. Often the Communications Manager of an organisation is chosen during crises, and is very successful. The most common problem with such an appointment of a crisis communication manager is that as the appointee is already an employee of the organisation, they will tend to have an organisational bias and consequently seek to defend the organisation and at times be tempted to use it as an opportunity to market the organisation. This distracts from solving the crisis and trying to maintain the organisation's reputation, and risks being perceived as ego centric. When there is no suitable communications staff available for the crisis manager role, it is often more sensible and efficient to hire a public relations consultant who only specialises in reputational crises.

7.4 The Crisis Communications Centre

A crisis communications (call) centre is to provide a single point of contact for the media, other stakeholders, and the public. The news media will try to contact the organisation to get more information but it does not make sense for the person/s in charge of actually dealing with the crisis to spend all their time answering questions from journalists. A lot of this information can be provided by other staff as often it will not be information critical to the crisis, but more general information to provide background and context. As such, a crisis communications centre does not necessarily have to be completely comprised of communications staff.

Crisis communications centre staff could be sourced more many areas from within the organisation, for the main requirement here is for the staff to be able to answer calls, emails, and online queries. For the purposes of a check list, crisis communications centre staff should be able to;

- Represent the organisation's ethos and image
- Communicate clearly and efficiently
- Deal with callers who are frustrated, angry, or anxious
- Refer the caller or advise the caller that their enquiry will be answered with a return call (or escalate the call to the crisis manager if critical)
- Collect relevant data (if any) from callers

The main objective of the crisis communication call centre staff is to be the public's single point of contact so that other parts of the organisation can continue as much as possible with day to day operations.

To ensure that all crisis communication call centre staff communicates externally correctly, it makes sense to develop 'scripted' answers for anticipated questions. It is not possible to anticipate and script answers for every possible question that may arise, and for questions that cannot be answered from the script, the question should be escalated to the call centre manager. Often it is easier for call centre staff to have a decision tree to follow so that they can find the correct answer quickly.

Requirements
Due to the logistical requirements of a crisis communication call centre in terms of staffing, information technology requirements (such as email, access to the organisation's social media, telephone connections, and so forth, it is sensible to develop plans before a crisis occurs and regularly update these plans. The crisis communications call centre should have:

- Adequate, suitable, and planned staffing for 24 h cycles
- Computers and technology set up so the staff can access and manage:
  - Email
  - Telephone connections
  - Social media

7.5 Dealing with Affected or Aggrieved Stakeholders

As crises can take any form, it is not practical to list each potential affected or aggrieved stakeholder that could be impacted by a crisis that has not yet happened. However, it makes sense to prepare for a situation whereby stakeholders are injured, or worse killed. Not only will those stakeholders need tending to, their relatives and partners will need to be informed, and dealt with in the most delicate and understanding matter. These persons should be contacted directly by the organisation immediately. It is the decent thing to do, and it also allows for the crisis manager to allocate sufficient human resources to what will be an extremely personal interaction. For that reason, the staff allocated to this task need to be selected very carefully and thoughtfully.

It is important that these stakeholders be dealt with honestly. Any deviation from the truth will likely come out in future, and will almost definitely start a new crisis. Suffice to say that the staff conducting these calls will need to be briefed quickly yet carefully. These staff will also need to be managed to make sure that all stakeholders are called as they should and no mistakes are made. These stakeholders will be in a fragile state. It is important to contact them so they don't have to try to find out their loved ones are affected. Future contact details and plans for these stakeholders should be pre-determined so that they will know when to hear from the organisation again, as to manage their expectations and give them some sense of stability of knowing what is next in this new process (Harvard Business School, 2009).

Although dealing with reputational crises is an organisational matter, dealing with people who have been affected can easily be a very sensitive matter.

7.6 Crisis Fixed – Ten Steps to Effective Crisis Resolution

1. Acknowledge that the offending act has happened*
2. Acknowledge pain*
3. Form a crisis panel and crisis communications centre
4. Understand the offensiveness*
5. Apologize for the event and express empathy
6. Communicate corrective action plan to avoid extending further impact from the event
7. Communicate prevention plan. Go beyond legislative requirements and stakeholder expectations.
8. Update media and stakeholders on points 6 and 7, and compensation payments. Reiterate points 1, 2, 4, and express empathy.
9. Seek satisfied comments from the previously offended and/or aggrieved, and publicise these.
10. Lead industry in prevention.

*Note – some of the first steps are internal processes in that they should be enacted without the media presence. Acknowledging that the offending act has happened means that you understand and have come to terms that it has happened, and that it can be communicated with others within the organisation (though only for the purpose of limiting any further impacts and managing the crisis). Acknowledging the pain or suffering is partly an internal personal process of coming to understand that there are some people who have experienced pain or suffering as a result of the offending act. Similarly, understanding the offensiveness is also an internal personal process about coming to terms with the idea that people are genuinely offended by the crisis causing act. These first internal steps are precursors to dealing with the media and other stakeholders so that you can respond to those issues in a genuine manner. Some stakeholders are already upset by the offending act occurring, it would only make things worse if you come across as disingenuous when apologizing or when acknowledging that the offending act occurred.

Whilst you are processing these first steps internally, establish a crisis panel and crisis communications centre. The following explains these steps in some detail.

Step 1. Acknowledge That the Offending Act Has Happened
Following Benoit's notion that the organisation is being held to account, the media and social media already have determined that an offending act has taken place, and that the organisation is being held to account. Regardless of who *should* be held to account, it makes sense to acknowledge that the offending act has happened, as most publics are informed by the media, it is capricious to deny what the publics already perceive to be true.

Step 2. Acknowledge the Pain
Seek to genuinely understand the pain experienced by offended/affected stakeholders. These people have been offended on a deep level (otherwise they would not have been as vocal as they have been. Anyone who is willing to oust a large organisation with significant financial resources and likely an equally large legal team is definitely upset). Though it may be difficult to understand the pain exactly as it is experienced by the stakeholder/s, it helps when you can acknowledge the pain through the media, and directly to those stakeholders.

Step 3. Form a Crisis Panel and Crisis Communications Centre
If you haven't already done so, form a crisis panel as soon as possible. In the fast moving environment of a crisis, it may be difficult to create a formal panel, but work with what you can have. Most offended and aggrieved stakeholders would be interested in an opportunity to express their grief to you in this forum. The crisis panel should remain active during the crisis to develop satisfactory outcomes, and post crisis to facilitate the development of best practice methods for the industry.

The Crisis Communications Centre is for inbound queries and outbound communications with the media and other stakeholders. Simply a press and public relations communication centre established to update online communications, distribute media statements, to answer calls from authorities and people seeking to clarify information regarding the impacts and wellbeing of others who may have been affected by the crisis causing act.

Step 4. Understand the Offensiveness and Apologise for Pain and Offensiveness
Be it that lives have been lost, someone has been discredited, or somewhere in between, it is reasonable to be expected to understand the offensiveness of the act. It may be difficult to see it from your own point of view. However the crisis is not about your own point of view. The crisis exists because stakeholders are offended, and even if you cannot wholly see the act as offensive as the stakeholders will, it is critical at this stage to understand why it was seen as offensive. Apologize for the pain and offensiveness through the media, and to the stakeholders directly (most crisis literature will steer away from this, as normally legal staff advice not to take ownership).

Step 5. Apologize for the Event and Express Empathy
The crisis is an event, in which an offending act has taken place, and the organisation is being held to account for it. Thus in the public's view, the organisation is guilty. Since the accusation of guilt already exists, it makes sense to apologize for the event. In many situations, an organisation's legal team will advise against

apologizing for the event, for it could open the doors to litigation as many could sue the organisation for loss and/or damages and have a massive financial impact on the organisation. However there is a difference between apologizing for an event, and legally taking responsibility for it. From a legal perspective, you can apologize that the actual event has taken place, and that people were adversely affected and show empathy for those affected, without admitted liability. In other words instead of saying "we are sorry for causing the explosion", you can instead say "we are sorry the explosion happened". Apologizing for pain and offensiveness does not mean that your organisation is assuming responsibility. Instead it means that you and your organisation are compassionate and have empathy[1].

The following sample media statement uses this strategy, allowing for an expressing of empathy, without legal admission of liability.

> *We are sorry that the* [insert event. For instance "explosion"] *has taken place. Our hearts are with those who are* [adversely affected. For instance "are mourning for their loved ones"]. *Everyone in our organisation,* [insert organisation name] *is saddened by the event and can at best only imagine the suffering. We are organising our resources to support those affected to the best of our ability, and will have made progress with* [insert actionable resource allocation and use]. *We are working with our stakeholders, specifically* [insert salient stakeholder group/types names] *to rectify the current situation, and make sure this can never happen again in our industry. We will update you at* [insert time], *later today.*

(This sample media statement is approximately 140 words only, because many news media articles are around 300 words. This means the news media can add background without having to reduce the statement. The shorter sentences lend themselves to being used in headlines, as well as social media quotes).

Step 6. Communicate Corrective Action Plan to Avoid Extending Further Impact from the Event

This is easily the most intuitive step as it is mostly a reflex action, and stakeholders will support it. Be it the temporary shutting down of leaking oil infrastructure, the temporary shutting down of faulty production lines, or the terminating a work function of an executive, until the situation has been addressed, revised, and improved. Resources will have to be allocated to the shutdown, and likely financial markets will react negatively towards the reduction of output. However the financial markets are more likely to react favourable to the temporary shutdown if it is explained that it will limit the damages caused by the event. If the media statement announcing the temporary shutdown includes mentions of revising the causes of the issue, and improving the methods to be the industry best, the financial market's reaction may be neutral. Taking a progressive and decisive step amidst the chaos of a reputational crisis is indicative of strong, focussed, and ethical leadership that will place the organisation well to lead the industry in the future. Though it may appear

[1] Perhaps one of the bigger problems in crisis communication research publications is that rarely, if ever, the stakeholder's feelings are met empathy. Instead, researchers propose "communication strategies" in the most clinical manner. Although some level of abstraction from feelings may help in making business decisions, as opposed to emotional responses, it is counter-productive to not pay homage to the feelings of the offended and aggrieved.

counterintuitive, if the financial markets depreciate the company's share price resulting from the possibility of fines, compensation, and other financial liabilities, the post crisis share price will be more likely to be stable and/or grow as the financial uncertainty has already been taken into account by those financial markets. It's when the financial markets have to work in the uncertainty of unknown fines and financial liabilities that the share price can remain volatile, which can lead to the further restrictions and enduring impact on the corporation.

Step 7. Communicate Prevention Plan. Go Beyond Existing Legislative Requirements and Stakeholder Expectations

It is fair to say that you can't please everyone, but it is reasonable to appease those salient stakeholders affected by the crisis. Oftentimes stakeholders will see genuine remorse and possibly empathy when one takes corrective action. More so when they see you take preventative measures to ensure the same offensive act won't happen again in the future. Therefore it makes sense to work with the stakeholders in a crisis panel that will have positive outcomes that satisfies most, if not all, salient stakeholders. An effective crisis panel will contribute to the following outcomes;

(a) Ensure that the event won't happen again, across the industry
(b) Show empathy, in part through showing commitment to safeguarding future and current stakeholders from similar events
(c) Show leadership by taking responsibility of the event outcomes by making sure all salient stakeholders participate in the crisis panel
(d) Show corporate social responsibility by taking ownership of the organisation in the context of society and the environment in which the organisation operates.
(e) Temper shareholder expectations through committing to resolving the crisis, limiting the financial liabilities, and leading the industry through constructive improvements.
(f) Gain support from the stakeholders who will promote your organisation's commitment and corporate social responsibility and likely call out anyone in your industry who does not commit to better preventative standards and measures.
(g) Regain trust from the public and stakeholders through effective positive stakeholder inclusion and stakeholder communication with the news media.
(h) Develop a framework likely to be used in forthcoming legislative changes.

When your organisation does take the progressive steps to develop and live up to the best practice standards to ensure a similar offensive event won't happen again in the future, likely it will lead to significant pressure being placed on your industry competitors. As salient stakeholders will begin to applaud your progressive actions, they and the news media will look at other organisations in the industry for a likelihood of a similar event occurring, and publicly hold those other organisations to account for not safeguarding against a preventable offensive event. Post crisis news media rhetoric will often include responses from politicians on proposals to increase legislation to prevent such future events. In plain terms, after the crisis, news media will often extend their crisis story by having a witch hunt for organisations that do not make a good effort to improve standards to prevent more offensive events.

An effective crisis panel is very influential in developing future safeguarding legislation and its terms of reference. This has significant value in the post crisis stage as it allows your organisation to establish the industry bench marks.[2]

Step 8. Update Media and Stakeholders on Points 5 and 6, and Compensation Payments. Reiterate Points 1, 2, and 4 [Insert Key Message Therein]
The number one rule of crisis communication strategy taught in universities is that the organisation should always communicate with the media;

(a) Immediately when the event has taken place to:

- Acknowledge the event
- Express concern and empathy
- Minimize further impact. (such as recalls or evacuation instructions)
- Provide a summary of the event
- Provide a time of next media statement (usually within 4 h of this first media statement. Normally in this first media statement question most won't be answered due to lack of information, with the exception of questions relating to minimizing further impact such as evacuations or safety instructions).

(b) Four hours after initial media statement, to

- Instruct on evacuation/product recall
- Request assistance (if relevant)
- Alleviate concern regarding
  - Extent of impact on affected stakeholders
  - Unaffected areas of the business
  - Unaffected stakeholders
- Manage the information flow
- Manage framing the crisis (within the bounds of the context of the crisis)
- Gain support of salient stakeholders
- Ask salient stakeholders to help through a crisis panel
- Provide news media with information packet (see the next chapter)

---

[2] A lot of very large corporations get this wrong and miss tremendous opportunity. For example, the then BP CEO was hauled to the White House during the BP Deepwater Horizon crisis to explain what they were doing. The company should have pre-empted this using a crisis panel (in part to inform the White House) and played a key role in developing future legislation designed to safeguard against these events.

Similarly, Facebook was required to appear before a Congressional Hearing to explain its actions related to its role in the Cambridge Analytica reputational crises. A crisis panel would have ensured that the relevant authorities were kept informed (albeit confidentially), and played a key role in developing legislation to guard against data misuse.

Instead, both BP and Facebook were basically told to sit outside whilst their political masters not only determined their fines, but also designed the rules that would have a significant impact on their future operations, further destabilising share prices.

Subsequent media statements should be regular, and at expected intervals. Salient crisis stakeholders who are not privy to information can quickly escalate the crisis further by calling the organisation experiencing the crisis as secretive and withholding critical information. For further details and sample media statements see the next chapter.

Step 9. Seek Satisfied Comments from the Previously Offended and/or Aggrieved, and Publicise These

It would be best if previously aggrieved or offended stakeholder made positive media statements on their own volition. Bear in mind though, that they may be too busy rebuilding their lives after the crisis to bother with making positive statements about an organisation that "destroyed" their lives in the first place.

Should this be the case, your most accessible source for quotes, statements, or at the very some anecdotal information about how the crisis was handled, will be the crisis panel. The stakeholder's representatives in the crisis panel should consist of aggrieved stakeholders, legislators, interest groups, news media, politicians, and so forth. These stakeholders already have a significant following amongst their peers, and some are leaders for their groups. Thus not only can the crisis panel help you get out of the crisis, if they are inclined to do so,[3] they may be instrumental in rebuilding your reputation and ensuring that the future is tangible and prosperous for your organisation.

By the nature of news media and their respective news values (what makes news), the positive outcomes of the crisis will make great news stories. Stakeholder's accounts of how they endured suffering, and helped to make sure that the offensive event can't happen again, will make for good news headlines. Likely they will be thrilled with the idea of having had an active role in the recovery process and how they helped resolve issues. If the crisis panel was handled well these previously aggrieved stakeholders will now champion the end result.

Step 10. Lead Industry in Prevention

Going from a bad situation to leading the industry in prevention may sound like a very ambitious path. Most certainly if the organisation has experienced a reputational crisis it was possibly operating at a level below the average standards. Hence for it to become the best in the industry, it is a large leap.

However who is better placed to understand how to prevent a crisis? Be it that the crisis was one of ethical conduct, the organisation would be useful in helping changing legislation and industry practices, as the organisation knows exactly where the loopholes were. If the crisis were like that of Top Gear, with Jeremy Clarkson and the BBC held to account for his alcohol fuelled tantrums, who would be better than Jeremy Clarkson to use the platform of the show for the last 2 min of each episode to talk about how the treatment for alcohol abuse is going? Would BP not have the some of the most comprehensive knowledge on where the risks are for Deepwater oil exploration platforms? Would Facebook not know how much data commercialisation is too much, and abuse of privileges? The list could go on for pages and pages

[3] If the crisis panel discussions were properly held and egalitarian and stakeholders were satisfied with the outcomes, it is reasonable to think that this is an acceptable request.

with organisations that were perfectly placed, and in the limelight, not only to make their organisation the best and most trusted in preventative measures, but also to lead their industry to new standards of social, economic, environmental accountability and responsibility.

The below diagram (Fig. 7.7) sets out different pathways available during different stages of a reputational crises.

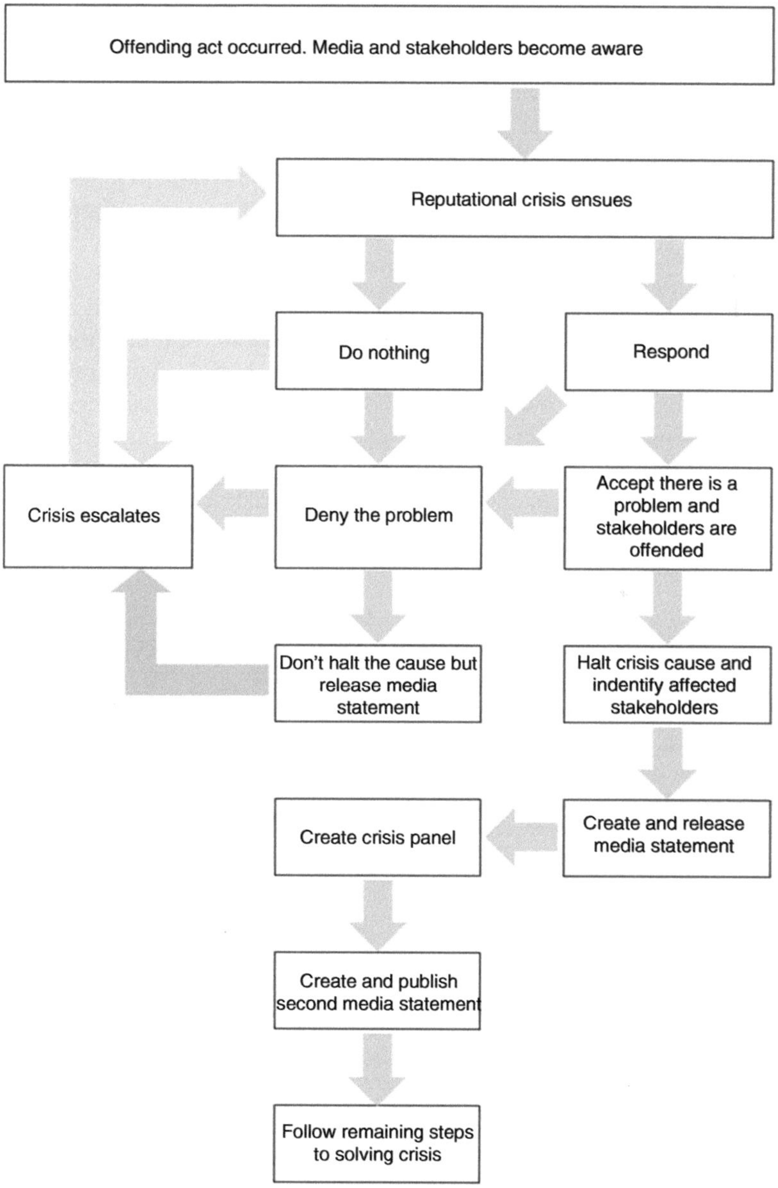

Fig. 7.7 Reputational crisis action flow chart

7.6.1 Summary

Crisis communication strategies and actions cannot be separated in practical terms. Although in research these two fields are handled completely separately, it has little relevance to practical application. Simply because it is all good and well to say the right thing, but then to not deliver on that will cause even more problems. Similarly, to do the right thing and not communicate it might fix the problem, but it won't stop the crisis as many uninformed stakeholder will still be offended.

Furthermore, to suggest that a type of communication strategy can be so effective that only communicating something can solve a crisis is mostly insulting to the organisation and its stakeholders. Thus reputational crisis actions and communications must go hand in hand, to solve the problem and to communicate the solution to those affected and other stakeholders.

This notion of best practice in crisis communication and resolution might be critiqued to be oversimplified as it does not detail stakeholder specifics, or all types of crisis situations.

The number of different types of reputational crises that can occur is unlimited. And if this weren't so and every crisis type had a particular solution, then we could learn from these lists of solutions to avoid reputational crises, and reputational crises would not exist at all. As this is not the case, it is best to take a mode generic approach to fixing the crisis by doing the right thing (since being perceived as doing the wrong thing caused the crisis).

This model directly engages with what makes a crisis a crisis. That is; offended stakeholders. This model also does take into account the various stakeholder dynamics and is generic enough to be useful in any type of reputational crisis.

Conclusion

The Chinese symbol for crisis is composed of two characters; danger and opportunity. The danger element you are well aware of. But too often we don't stop to think that each crisis presents the opportunities to meet with your stakeholders and work with them. Each crisis helps you understand your strengths and weaknesses. Most importantly, each crisis gives you the opportunity to lead your industry by developing a best practice standard to ensure it won't happen again. If you don't take the reins, someone else will.

7.7 Media Statement Templates

The following media statement templates are provided to be used as a framework. Different statements are suitable for different times during reputational crises. Due to the nature of reputational crises being unique, and each having unique stakeholders and situations, it is impossible to develop a media statement that fits perfectly for every crisis situations. The below may be used as they are, however they will likely need some customisation to be effective for any crisis specifics.

General Instructions for Media Statements

- Always have the same person deliver the media statements. Be it the CEO, Communications manager, head of operations, or a crisis communication consultant. Consistency is crucial as it helps meet expectations and in part consistency helps bring about the notion of reliability and stability.[4]
- Media statements should be delivered by someone with a high level of authority who can make decision regarding the crisis.
- Post your media statements online with your organisation's website (on the main landing page) and on your social media accounts, so that they can be verified by news media and others.
- Provide staff with the media statement as it is being released. This not only helps calm staff and aids in managing their expectations, but is also helpful for ensuring the message is consistent throughout the organisation. It might be wise to provide staff with further background to the crisis, when applicable. For example, front line staff will need to be briefed on how to handle customer concerns regarding the extent of the damage and/or risk, as well as how the organisation will safeguard from future events.
- Your media statements may in part or at times completely be designed for a select group of stakeholders. However, other stakeholders will receive the message and judge you on how you are dealing with those stakeholders. That is to say, your communication's intended target audience may be a few, but your communications will be reviewed by many.
- If you need to answer questions or develop your own statements, a few simple rules to bear in mind are;
  - People don't care what you say until you say you care.
  - People are more important than the environment and property
  - The environment and property is more important than money.

7.7.1 Initial Media Statement

Timing

- Immediately when adequate information is available the first media statement should be released. You only need to know the; what, where, and when details of the incident. The "why" isn't expected of you at this stage. The "who" of who is affected is helpful, but specifics are not critical at this early stage. The news media may speculate and publish why the event happened, but they are unlikely to speculate and publish who specifically was affected.

[4] Leunig (2005) posits that instincts and morality are rarely compatible, leading to a notion of unreliable imagery. "It may well be the case that motorcycle gangs are about the only organisations worthy of public trust these days… In Freudian terms, the id and the superego are fused blissfully (and miraculously) together and the situation is sweetly conflicted" (Leunig, 2005).

Of course, if a specific group of people are affected, it is reasonable name the group, without going into specifics but do not name persons affected.

- Do not waste anyone's time. The media and stakeholders need to see that you are busy with managing the crisis, and not just waiting around for something to happen or make small talk with the media. The news media reporters are in a rush as they are trying to beat each other to be the first to release the story. They have to get their story published immediately.

Purpose of Initial Media Statement

- To instruct on safety/evacuation/product recall
- To request assistance (if relevant)
- To alleviate concern regarding;
  - Extent of impact on affected stakeholders
  - Unaffected areas of the business
  - Unaffected stakeholders
- To manage the information flow. If you don't provide the information for the news media, they will find it. Even worse, if they can't find it, they will likely speculate. This is the first and the most important opportunity to frame the crisis to manage it effectively.
- If possibly, frame the story within the bounds of the crisis. In other words, stop the story from affecting other non-affected stakeholders or other parts of the organisation.

First Media Statement Template

> *We confirm that* [insert event] *has taken place today at* [insert time] *at* [insert location]. *We have taken steps to immediately to eliminate the risk of the situation spreading and we are working with the authorities and stakeholders to address the main priorities now. We will soon have further information to determine the extent of the* [event]. *In the meantime, please avoid* [use of location/product/service].
>
> *We are sorry that the* [insert event. For instance "contamination"] *has taken place. Our hearts are with those who are* [adversely affected. For instance "are mourning for their loved ones"]. *Everyone here at* [insert organisation name*] is saddened by the event and can at best only imagine the suffering.*
>
> *We are organising our resources to support those affected, and will have made progress with* [insert actionable resource allocation and use]. *We are establishing a* crisis call centre *to help answer questions. It will be operational in 30 minutes. The contact details will be available on our website and social media shortly.*
>
> *We are working with authorities and our stakeholders, specifically* [insert salient stakeholder's names/groups] *to rectify the current situation, and make sure this can never happen again in our industry. We will update you at* [insert time], *later today.*

7.7.2 Second Media Statement

Timing

- Between 2 and 4 h of initial media release, unless critical information becomes available earlier. If critical information becomes available earlier, adapt the media release to include the latest critical information. In such instance, it may be appropriate to issue the second media release earlier than planned.

Purpose of Second Media Statement

- Instruct and update on evacuation/product recall
- Request assistance (if relevant)
- Alleviate concerns regarding
  - Extent of impact on affected stakeholders
  - Unaffected areas of the business
  - Unaffected stakeholders
- Express empathy (and remorse if applicable and your legal team allows it)
- Manage the information flow
- Manage framing the crisis (within the bounds of the context of the crisis)
- Gain support of salient stakeholders to help solve the problem
- Ask salient stakeholders to help through a crisis panel to make sure it can't happen again
- Provide contact details of crisis call centre
- Provide news media with information packet (see next section)

Second Media Statement Template

> *We are updating to confirm that* [insert event] *has taken place today at* [insert time] *at* [insert location]. *We have taken steps to immediately to eliminate the risk of the situation spreading and we have established a working group with authorities and stakeholders and are addressing main priorities now.*
>
> *We are sorry that the* [insert event. For instance "contamination"] *has taken place. Our hearts are with those who are* [adversely affected. For instance "are mourning for their loved ones"]. *Everyone here at* [insert organisation name] *is saddened by the* [event or event impact] *and can at best only imagine the suffering.*
>
> *We have already directed some resources to assist those affected. To limit the* [event] *impact to other area we are mobilising other resources to assist with the recovery. We have established a* crisis call centre *to help answer questions. It is now operational and can be reached on* [insert number]. *Further details are available on our website and social media.*
>
> *We respectfully ask from our stakeholders, those affected by this event, and those who could be affected in future, to work with us to make sure this type of event will never happen again in our organisation and in our industry. We are working with authorities and our stakeholders, specifically* [insert salient stakeholder's names/groups] *to rectify the current situation, and make sure this can never happen again in our industry. We will update you at* [insert time], *later today.*

7.7.3 Social Media and Updates

Social media is a useful tool for updating news media on specifics of an ongoing crisis. However if you have supplied all critical and relevant material in a drip feed manner through social media, the news media is more likely to construct their own version of events, and not as likely to give priority to your official media statements.

Social media has its advantages. However one should exercise caution when using it, particularly during a reputational crisis. It is very easy during tense situations to have a statement misconstrued or to be caught up in defending accusations. Furthermore, due to the increase in public and stakeholder interest resulting from the crisis, it is likely that comments, posts, and feedback will quickly reach a point where it is impossible for the normal communications team to handle, both in volume and crisis communications skills and strategies. For example, a few years ago during an anti halal certification campaign led by organised social media based interest groups, Cadbury (United Kingdom) and Byron Bay Cookies Facebook pages received comments (including threats) at a rate of more than 1000 per hour.

In these instances, even the most seasoned social media specialists are overrun by the volume and after an hour of being attacked in this manner is likely to lose their ability to remain objective and unaffected. In such circumstances, it is best to call in a crisis communication consultant, who as an external party to the proceedings can remain objective.

Frequency of Updates – Keeping Stakeholders Informed

It is a good precaution to maintain a reliable and regular stream of updates, both on social media and through media statements. During the initial period, social media and news media will be hungry for content as the story is just developing and everyone wants to be the first to break the news. As the crisis continues, some news media organisations and stakeholders will seek to keep the story trending at the top of media. However as time progresses, readers and social media consumers will lose interest, unless there is a significant development. To ensure you maintain authority on what is going on with the crisis, you must maintain regular updates at intervals that the media and stakeholders can depend on. For instance, the crisis could escalate again if stakeholders feel they are left in the dark and the organisation hasn't said anything. In such an instance, the stakeholders will likely feel aggrieved and air their complaints and concerns with the news media, which will again raise the profile of the crisis to create news media content and inform their audience of the concerns.

Photos and Videos

The news media, stakeholders, and public are likely to add their own photos and videos online. However posting photos and videos online using the company's social media accounts is an effective means to developing the framing of the crisis. Oftentimes social media photos and videos do not completely tell a story, and the quality is likely to be of less quality as it was taken impromptu. Therefore the news media is more likely to use quality footage from your organisation's website and social media accounts.

7.7.4 *News Media Organisations*

The press is going to come to you with questions and continuously request updates. Despite the trending social media stories, the news media organisations still have a lot of influence over which news stories will headline for the day. Hence it makes good sense to keep them on your side. To make this easier, you should consider sharing a number of quality photos and video footage with news media organisations only.

News Media Information Packet
Develop an information packet before a crisis. This information packet will make it easier for the news media to develop their stories, particularly if they decide to develop editorials, or seek to determine how the crisis evolved. They will find all this information if they look for it anyway, thus it is best to give them the information willingly and proactively to let them know you have nothing to hide. Show that you are keen to work with them. The information packet should include:

- Crisis media contact details within your organisation
- Historical information such as organisation's growth since establishment
- Quantitative information such as number of current employees, turnover, locations of operations/branches
- Schematic of operational roles
- List of executives and Board of Directors
- Organisation's ethos. Including mission statement, organisational values, corporate objectives, and corporate social responsibility projects.
- Organisation's safety record
- Organisation's quality assurance
- Ethical standards and records

Try to not share these on social media or through your website (with the exception of the information packet) as the press may be inclined to use their own materials, including quotes, photos, and videos, which might not place your organisation in the best light. The focus here is work with the press, to help them help you.

Further Media Statements
Nearly always a reputational crisis will require more than two media statements. Once again, crisis specifics vary so significantly that it is not practical to more consecutive develop templates. Instead, the above two templates should suffice to develop a framework of what is needed going forth. If in doubt, acquire the services of a reputational crisis communications consultant to assist with customisation.

7.8 Summary – How to Fix Reputational Crises Whilst Leading the Industry Ethically

Some of the largest companies have experienced reputational crises during the past decade. The most notable western companies include British oil giant, BP. The automotive industry was also plagued with reputational crises ranging from Takata airbags that didn't deploy but were installed in tens of millions of cars across the world (National Highway Traffic Safety Administration, 2020). A Tesla autopilot car killed a pedestrian (Guardian Staff and Agencies, 2018), and Toyota had the problem of some cars accelerating on their own (Cowan, 2014). But in terms of reputational crises, Volkswagen really pushed their luck when the company was found to have tweaked their diesel cars to register lower than actual carbon emissions readings, defrauding authorities and consumers alike (SEC, 2019).

The aerospace sector had its share of reputational crises with Malaysian airlines losing two passenger jets in two separate incidents. The Malaysian Air flight MH370 simply went missing with passengers and crew never being heard from again (Scruton et al., 2017), and flight MH17 blew up over the Ukraine (it was later concluded that this flight was shot down) (BBC News, 2019). Also in the aerospace sector, Boeing took a numbers of hits on its previously strong reputation with design issues stated as the cause of crashes of the company's 737 Max passenger jet (BBC Staff, 2020).

A summative review and analysis of the print media of selected reputational crises (BP and Volkswagen) (both crises being partly attributable to CEO's not showing they cared about their societies and environments) did not reveal any significant references to social responsibility or trust. This is despite both CEO's openly declaring during the crises that they were doing the right thing, despite the crisis stakeholders being more adversely affected.

In terms of media coverage with the BP and Volkswagen reputational crises, there appeared to have been little focus on the CEO's trying to do the right thing and significant media focus on the sensational aspects of the stories. With these both crises the media focus was on environmental impacts and stakeholder impacts. According to the media accounts, the CEOs did not quickly try to do the right thing and limit crisis impacts to stakeholders through arresting the crisis cause and look after stakeholders. Overwhelmingly the share price impacts of crises appear to be a calculation based on the likely fines payable, restrictive trading, and compensation calculations. In other words, the crises caused impacts on their financial position and changes to operating practices. In terms of being held to account, media coverage of neither crises included much on corporate social responsibility or trust. In other words, there were virtually no utterances of the companies doing the right thing.

Perhaps the US$108 billion BP lost in value during the nadir of the Deepwater Horizon crisis (Sabet et al., 2012) would have been less if the CEO sought to focus on doing the right thing in terms of the environment and the affected stakeholders. For example, if the BP CEO was solely focussed on stopping the leaking oceanic oil well, the company may have gained support from all manner of global experts and brought the problem to a quick close. Similarly, the Volkswagen CEO could have funded and established a speedy enquiry into the emissions measures tampering and within a short time taken ownership of the findings and committed to fixing the issues and developing a best practice Volkswagen based testing company to which all the industry could be measured with (for if Volkswagen knew how to beat the system, they would be well placed to advise on how to make it unbeatable).

Taking crisis arresting measures can have the positive impact of inspiring stakeholders who want to assist the company by not lodging compensations claims or smaller claims at least. When the company tries to do the right thing immediately and the CEO stands to account of the company's actions publically, it is less likely that stakeholders and media will focus on punishing the company for intentional or unintentional offensive behaviour. It is more likely the stakeholders and media will instead focus on resolving the issue as quick as possible. Consequently there would a reduction in the amount of fines, compensation, and restrictive operating measures as legislators, suppliers, customers and resellers quickly regain confidence in the company's good intentions.

In terms of fiduciary duty to the company shareholders, this crisis strategy must be given due consideration, not once, but repeatedly throughout the crisis as the crisis stakeholders, crisis elements, and financial situations evolve.

Positive crisis communication and strategy should focus on:

1. Halting the offensive act
2. Standing to account for one's actions and empathy
3. Solving the problem
4. Fixing damages
5. Preventing future incidents in the industry (this shows concern for society and environment)

7.9 Limitations, Obstacles, and Concerns

The idea of redesigning the use of stakeholder theory likely will seem flawed as it is held as useful construct and used in companies that have since generated billions in profits. Yet, as discussed, even the largest of companies are often not able to deal with reputational crises or stakeholders effectively.

The proposition that a company itself becomes a stakeholder in a crisis, alongside the company's own stakeholders may appear from the company's perspective as a redistribution of power and influence at best, and as defeatist at worst. However it must be remembered that reputational crises cannot exist without stakeholders, and in terms of the reputational crises existing, it must be held that the crisis cannot exist without the company either.

If we were to apply Freeman's (1984) rule that a stakeholder is a party that can affect the company, or be affected by the company, to this idea that the crisis is at the centre of a stakeholder map, then both the company and other stakeholders can be affected by the crisis and affect the crisis. It is then obvious that this rule still works, as stakeholders (including the company) can affect the crisis by increasing or decreasing the salience of the crisis. Similarly the stakeholders (including the company) can also be affected by the crisis extensively to the point of the company being dissolved or stakeholders becoming entirely obsolete (as stakeholders), but also through creating more revenue and/or salience for the company or more salience for the stakeholders. In other words, the rule that defines a stakeholder as one being able to affect or be affected by an entity remains valid and fits this model.

However none of these arguments solve the issue for the corporate executive who is legally bound to look after shareholder's interests, as in they must place the company's financial welfare before the needs and wants of all stakeholders. This means that the answer to dealing with a reputational crisis lies not in wrapping it up in glib words, but rather to viewing company stakeholders differently, and acting on that to end the crisis as soon as possible.

Post Crisis Stakeholder Map and Relationships

Following the end of the crisis, the crisis stakeholders will likely want to retain their place with the organisation through an adaption of the crisis panel. Mostly the crisis stakeholders who had sufficient salience to be part of the crisis panel during the crisis, will continue to have a recognizable level of salience after the crisis. Naturally the salience will have decreased after the crisis as the;

(a) Stakeholders have lost urgency,
(b) Stakeholders have lost some of their legitimacy as the crisis no longer exists, and
(c) Stakeholders would have lost some of their power as the media no longer entertains or promotes their ideas actively.

The post crisis stakeholder map may be effective following the more traditional schema with the organisation at the centre, enjoying a symbiotic relationship with its stakeholders. It is possible that some crisis stakeholders will take issue with what may be seen as 'cast aside' when they are no longer urgently required for input or assistance in the crisis panel. This may result in resentment, and possibly though unlikely, attempts by those stakeholders to rekindle the crisis. However more probably the crisis panel stakeholders will have agreed that the urgency of the crisis has passed and all matters have been dealt with in a satisfactory manner.

It would be wise to consider maintaining relationships with the crisis panel stakeholders to avoid future problems of the same kind occurring. Even if sufficient safe guards were developed during the crisis by the crisis panel, it would be foolish to assume that any organisation is immune from reputational crisis. Unless every element of the organisation and its operating environment remain the same, there will always be a risk of another reputational crisis. Hence it would be useful to have a consulting panel of the organisation's strongest and most outspoken critics. In summary, it would be wise to retain the salient crisis stakeholders who were active in the crisis panel to provide counsel, direction, and their voice legitimate concerns. For in all likelihood, another crisis may begin soon.

Overcoming Obstacles of a Decentralised Crisis Stakeholder Map
Changing the use of the contemporary stakeholder theory from being company centric to a more useful construct as a crisis centric model may well be viewed as a contentious modification. Joining the stakeholders around the table with the crisis at the centre could potentially result in a number of obstacles. The most foreseeable concerns of using are crisis panel are:

Stakeholders May Be Seen to Be More Powerful
Although stakeholders may be seen to be more powerful, this can have the positive effect of the stakeholders not feeling weak, and consequently not feeling frustrated, resentful, or subsequently angry. When people do not feel threatened or disempowered they are more likely to be open to suggestions, new ideas, and compromise.

(a) The organisation appears weaker

The organisation appears weaker than it is could have some company executives feeling disempowered or subjugated to stakeholders. However for there to be an egalitarian atmosphere in the discussions, everyone must feel that their opinions, objections, and principles matter. This may be a difficult proposition at times as some stakeholders may go as far as to suggest that it would be best if the company shut down. Likely such a suggestion would not have the support of other stakeholders (such as suppliers, staff, community beneficiaries and so forth) who are dependent on the survival of the company, and those supporting stakeholders would be expected to neutralise such extreme suggestions. In other words, in part at least, the strength of the company is made up by all its stakeholders.

Most importantly, company representative/s at the panel should have sufficient emotional intelligence to not be personally offended, aggrieved, or otherwise emotionally responsive to unfavourable situations and comments made in panel discussions. This means that selecting the correct company representative/s for the panel may be a somewhat difficult task as the task requires someone to have resilience, compassion, strength, openness, and high intelligence. Ideally the company representative/s would be able to think outside of the box (and normal operations). The company representative/s should also be able to lead the panel to a new direction when discussions become unproductive or circular.

(b) Corporate executives may struggle to place their executive duty (by law) to look after the shareholder's interests.

Corporate executives may struggle to place their executive duty (by law) to look after the shareholder's interests. The company representative/s must display sufficient empathy and consideration to all other stakeholders, however must do so without admitting financial liability, nor failing in a duty of care. The company's interest must be protected, and can be done whilst still treating afflicted stakeholder in a fair manner. One of the more long term objectives of the panel is to avoid costly and lengthy litigation, and this can be circumvented through carefully framing the issue, which is the crisis, not the company.

Company representative/s are legally bound to serve shareholder interests, it would be prudent to communicate that outset of panel discussions in a manner which does not stimulate ill-will in other stakeholder representatives. Throughout the course of panel discussions other stakeholder representative may need to be reminded that the company representatives are legally bound to protect their shareholders. This should deflect the problem from concerns or aggression by the other stakeholder representatives who should then accept it as a legally bound obligation, and refocus on the solving of the crisis. Stakeholder representatives might find this reasoning easier to digest if they are informed that everyone is there to solve the crisis, and to prevent such crisis reoccurring.

(c) Media focussed may be diffused, leading to less focus on what the company has to say, and stakeholders gaining a prevailing voice in the media.

Media focussed may be diffused, leading to less focus on what the company has to say, and stakeholder gaining a prevailing voice in the media. At first thought, this may be a problem because it suggests that company opposing stakeholders are being allowed to frame the crisis in the news media. However, the crisis already exists, and by nature of what a reputational crisis is, most likely the news media are already giving the opposing crisis stakeholders their attention. The construction of the panel is egalitarian which in this instance means that more vocal stakeholders are given the same importance as less vocal stakeholders, thereby reducing the denomination of new news media by any one particular stakeholder group.

The crisis panel arrangements should not be ongoing in as it was during the crisis. Only stakeholder committee meetings should be held after the crisis to ensure there is no repeat of the offending incident, and to work together with the company for mutual benefits.

Concerns About the Timeliness of a Crisis Panel to Develop Solutions

Reputational crises, like most other crises, are phenomena wherein urgency and timeliness is very important. Thus the idea of forming a crisis panel to discuss the pressing issues may seem to be counterintuitive because logistically it will take longer than an individual or an in-house counsel meeting to develop a solution. However it is similarly counterintuitive for that individual or in-house counsel to quickly develop potential solutions to the crisis and have that solution worsen the crisis as a result of not having enough input from salient stakeholders. In other words, speeding towards solutions may have the opposite effect of developing problems further.

Reputational crises sometimes are finished within hours of starting. But more often than not, reputational crises can be active for weeks and sometimes months. When reputational crises carry on for many weeks, stakeholders including suppliers, customers, and employees, tend to become nervous about the longevity of the organisation. In such situation, these stakeholders are likely to look toward other customers, suppliers, and employers that seem more stable.

Ongoing reputational crisis risks lead to reputational concerns and longevity of the organisation, and consequently are likely to follow with an exodus of stakeholders upon which the organisation relies. Hence it is obvious that reputational crises should be solved quickly and effectively, without risking making the crisis worse through insufficiently informed crisis mangers. In simple terms, crises need good solutions quickly, not potentially solutions immediately.

Concerns About the Ethos of the Crisis Panel
The notion of placing the problem (the crisis) at the centre and having the company as a stakeholder may seem novel and possibly naïve. However it is somewhat similar to the model that is a Board of Directors. Oftentimes these Boards represent the common interest of Directors (which is the company in normal circumstances, similar to stakeholders representing their common interest which is to change things to suit their priorities. The different individuals that make up the Board of Directors all represent various aspects that are important to the main objective. For example the Board would include a Director focussed on Finance, above all else. Another Director may be focussed on production, and yet another may have the role of ensuring the legal aspects of the company are well served. These positions are not at all dissimilar to the varying roles played by different representatives in a crisis panel. Although the crisis panel representatives do not all serve the same company as the Board of Directors does, the different crisis panel representatives do all serve the crisis panel objectives of wanting the crisis to be solved. The varying priorities of the representatives of the crisis panel would be argued as difficult to overcome, yet in the operations of a Board of Directors, the different Members of the Board similarly have varying priorities. From this viewpoint, it seems naïve that a company can be managed at its highest level through the Board of Directors panel, but when it comes to a reputational crisis, the idea of a panel with various representatives would be dismissed. Thus it seems counterintuitive to thwart the idea of a crisis panel operating similar to a Board of Directors.

In summary, there may be obstacles in using a panel of crisis stakeholders to solve reputational crises, but as a crisis cannot exist without stakeholders, then there must be more deference paid to stakeholders, and engaging with a stakeholder inclusive model. Although crisis communications in a strict sense only deals with the communications aspect of crises, it idealistic to think that mere communications alone can fix a crisis, as it is idealistic to think that actions without the right communications can fix a crisis. Reputational crises can be solved through communications and actions working hand in hand, as organisation can work hand in hand with their stakeholders.

7.10 Conclusion

Reputational crisis communication is a construct which like everything else is constantly evolving. This book covers some of the larger problems in both research and practice, including numerous examples of how crises could have been handled better.

The dependency of both industry and academia on older stakeholder theory has led crisis communication down a seemingly egotistic path whereby corporations seem to want to do anything to save themselves and stakeholders are simply a by-product of their business ventures. If there is any merit to society, the social contract, laws, and most of all the shared human condition, then corporations must play their role in being better citizens, and in return they can expect a more supporting citizenry.

Both research and industry mostly centre their efforts on blame, attribution, and basically what to say to get out of a sticky situation. A conversation on how to improve things is far more productive than trying to convince others that you are not entirely to blame. The media, for its own purposes does encourage sensationalism, and often looks for a party to blame. Most people would personally rather blame their woes on others, but a confident self-aware person listens, considers other's viewpoints, and then seeks to resolve the problem to mutual benefit.

A reputational crisis does not have to be exactly that. Although an organisation is held to account for doing the wrong thing, it does not need to negatively impact the organisation's reputation. Though often it happens that an organisation is held to account, the organisation denies it should be held to account and/or it hasn't done anything wrong, the stakeholders punish the organisation and set in place some new parameters so that the organisation's actions don't impact them or others negatively.

Instead, an organisation accused of an offending act can accept that it is being held to account for the act. It can then immediately denounce that act as a misstep, and call on stakeholders to help the organisation develop processes and systems to avoid it ever happening again. The organisation could then go from being known to one that commits offensive acts, to one that helps stop the industry from committing such offensive acts.

Now more than ever, we are in a competitive world. And in a more competitive world, succeeding demands higher standards. Why not take the opportunity to be regarded as the best!

Bibliography

BBC News. (2019, June 19). *MH17: Four charged with shooting down plane over Ukraine*. Retrieved January 20, 2020, from BBC World News: https://www.bbc.com/news/world-europe-48691488

BBC Staff. (2020, January 10). *Boeing faces fine for 737 Max plane 'designed by clowns'*. Retrieved January 20, 2020, from BBC Business News: https://www.bbc.com/news/business-51058929

Cowan, J. (2014, March 20). *Toyota to pay $1.3 billion for deadly defect cover-up*. Retrieved January 20, 2020, from ABC News: https://www.abc.net.au/news/2014-03-20/toyota-pays-1-3-billion-for-defect-cover-up-statements/5332894

Freeman, R. E. (1984). *Strategic management: A stakeholder approach*. Pitman Publishing.

Guardian Staff and Agencies. (2018, April 1). *Tesla car that crashed and killed driver was running on Autopilot, firm says*. Retrieved January 20, 2020, from The Guardian: https://www.theguardian.com/technology/2018/mar/31/tesla-car-crash-autopilot-mountain-view

Harvard Business School. (2009). *Managing through a crisis*. Harvard University Press.

Leunig, M. (2005). Foreword. In L. Gettler (Ed.), *Organisations behaving badly*. Wiley.

National Highway Traffic Safety Administration. (2020). *Takata recall spotlight*. Retrieved January 20, 2020, from NHTSA: https://www.nhtsa.gov/equipment/takata-recall-spotlight

Sabet, S., Cam, M., & Heaney, R. (2012). Sharemarket reaction to the BP oil spill and the US government moratorium on exploration. *Australian Journal of Management, 37*(1), 61–76.

Scruton, P., Phipps, C., & Levett, C. (2017, January 17). *Missing flight MH370 – A visual guide to the parts and debris found so far*. Retrieved January 20, 2020, from The Guardian: https://www.theguardian.com/world/ng-interactive/2017/jan/17/missing-flight-mh370-a-visual-guide-to-the-parts-and-debris-found-so-far

SEC. (2019, March 15). *SEC charges Volkswagen, former CEO with defrauding bond investors during "clean diesel" emissions fraud.* Retrieved April 15, 2020, from U.S. Securities and Exchange Commision: https://www.sec.gov/litigation/litreleases/2019/lr24422.htm

Chapter 8
Crisis Prevention

Abstract A reputational crisis without stakeholders is not a crisis, for without afflicted stakeholders, interest groups, politicians, or media, there is no one to hear of an offending action. This means that arguably stakeholders are as important as the company in a reputational crisis. Thus if we treat the stakeholder map accordingly, it will have an impact on crisis prevention.

Through employing this viewpoint, it becomes clearer that crisis prevention can be more focussed on stakeholders and that we can more effective in addressing the stakeholder related elements. For example; managing stakeholder relationships, stakeholder monitoring, media surveillance, and ethical data management. Each of these strategies will be enhanced through developing genuine relationships with stakeholders, and the organisation may likely benefit from having a strong opponent who will highlight potential reputational crises and operational pitfalls. Furthermore, employing these stakeholder orientated strategies will aid in reducing the likelihood of a crisis occurring, reduce the extent of crisis impacts, and creates good corporate governance practices through engaging with stakeholders and issues as they arise, or before they arise.

This chapter engages with the more holistic stakeholder strategy and employs it to improve effectiveness in reputational crises prevention. Stakeholder concerns, activities, and salience are brought into the equation to assist in managing reputational crisis prevention, building resilience, and develop a more engaging stakeholder management philosophy. This chapter summarizes the ethos of the preceding chapters and is more useful to be read before a reputational crisis occurs, than after a reputational crisis occurs.

The best way to manage a crisis is to avoid it naturally through dealing with issues effectively. Unfortunately good practices are naturally often forgotten, and tend to transmute as time progresses. Preventative practices to stave off reputational crises include;

T. Schermer, *Reputational Crises Unspun*, https://doi.org/10.1007/978-981-16-5130-4_8

- Managing stakeholder relationships
- Stakeholder monitoring
- Media surveillance
- Ethical data management

Employing all of these strategies in unison also gives a clear insight in how to increase operational performance and conduct. This next section discusses these strategies in some detail, and concludes with an overview on reputational crisis insurance.

8.1 Managing Stakeholder Relationships

As a crisis without stakeholders is not a crisis, it is important to understand your stakeholders before a crisis occurs. In developing a crisis prevention plan stakeholders should thus be the primary focus. There are many different types of stakeholder types, levels, and relationships. Although a stakeholder's salience may vary as a stakeholder's situations changes situation in terms of power, urgency, and legitimacy, it is good practice to understand these elements of as many stakeholders as possible.

Understanding a stakeholder's position in relation to your organisation can be critical in crisis prevention. It is important to know who are stakeholders are and what stakeholders want, and in crisis prevention, it is more important to know what they do not want. In crisis prevention it is useful to engage stakeholders in discussions with the view of understanding what their primary policies or objectives are, and then review with the stakeholders how they feel their policies/objectives relate to your organisation's policies, objectives, and operating procedures. Stakeholders can be very useful in understanding how other stakeholders who are external to the organisation view the organisation. Often stakeholders have a very different, yet legitimate view of your organisation, which may or may not be congruent with how the organisation likes to view itself because company employees and executives are more likely to provide complimentary feedback to the organisation that issues their pay checks and for which they have toiled away for a long time.

Understanding stakeholder perspectives prior to a crisis will aid significantly in preventing a crisis, but will also facilitate communications during a crisis. It is helpful to understand:

- What your stakeholders want
- What your stakeholders don't want
- How do the stakeholders view your organisation
- How can your organisation align itself more with the stakeholder's objectives?

Stakeholder salience is oftentimes a fluid construct as stakeholder's situations and their orientations towards your organisation are always in the state of flux. Therefore it is helpful to employ continues stakeholder reviews for your organisation, and engage with the stakeholders at a level where you can understand why they feel the way they do. That is to say; why do the stakeholders want what they want? What are the basis and/or motivations of their viewpoint and goals?

8.2 Stakeholder Monitoring

The term 'monitoring' may provoke some sinister connotations however the premise of stakeholder monitoring includes that a certain amount of distance, or objectivity, should be used to facilitate effectively understanding the stakeholders.

The task of monitoring stakeholders includes a variety of methods, as it is important to be able to understand the stakeholders in a variety of ways. Including but not limited to:

- Stakeholder objectives,
- Stakeholder motivations,
- Stakeholder viewpoints,
- Stakeholder salience (power, urgency, and legitimacy),
- Stakeholder relationships with the organisation, and
- Stakeholder relationships with other stakeholders.

Stakeholder Objectives are the primary concern for an organisation for if an organisation doesn't understand the stakeholder's end goals, then it is difficult for the organisation to (a) work with the stakeholder to help them achieve their objective, and (b) to make sure that objective isn't harmful to the organisation's reputation.

Stakeholder Motivations differ to the stakeholder's objectives as the motivations are the underlying sentiments that drive the stakeholder's motivations. For example, a stakeholder may have had a previous experience with a similar organisation that had negative impacts for them, and through communicating it may be possible to differentiate that previous experience to what the stakeholder is concerned about with your organisation. Additionally, a stakeholder's motivations based on a previous experience might be useful in developing an insight into a specific situation that could be risky for both the stakeholder and the organisation. In most instances, stakeholders with concerns will be happy to explain their motivations in great detail if asked.

Stakeholder Viewpoints are different to motivations and objectives for viewpoints are concerned with how the stakeholders see the organisation and potential issues. Stakeholder's viewpoints may vary within stakeholder groups. Though they share an affiliation and a common objective, their varying viewpoints may inform the organisation of different causes of concern with varying degrees of risk.

Stakeholder Salience is a critical factor in dealing with stakeholders when time is compressed during a reputational crisis. Thus it is more effective to determine who is who and why before a crisis begins. As discussed in the stakeholder chapter, stakeholder salience can be determined through understanding the power, urgency, and legitimacy of stakeholders. Outside of crisis situations urgency is less likely to be a factor. (For a more in-depth understanding of stakeholder salience, please see Chapter Three on stakeholders.) However it is important to remember that stakeholder's power, urgency, and legitimacy are in a state of flux, and as such, the stakeholder's salience will keep changing, creating the need for continues monitoring.

Stakeholder Relationships with the Organisation can also be in a state of flux as the level and type of engagement that the stakeholder has with the organisation can keep changing. To aid in preventing a reputational crisis, it is helpful to encourage honest and open communication with the stakeholders to be able to determine if the relationship is (a) improving or declining, and (b) if the stakeholder is becoming more or less engaged with the organisation.

Stakeholder's Relationships with Other Stakeholders can drastically change the salience of stakeholders. As explained in Chapter Three, an allegiance between stakeholders can increase their power, urgency, and legitimacy, all and at once. Changes in relationships between stakeholders can be an indication of the organisation being seen more or less favourable, and also is an effective indicator in determining the likelihood of a crisis. For example, a newly formed allegiance of stakeholders is often one of the key indicators that the stakeholders have a common concern and objective, which have become more salient. It would be prudent to engage with those stakeholders to fully understand their underlying motivations, with the view of reducing their concerns through either dealing with the issue of their concern, or contextualising the issue so that it is no longer a concern.

In summary, there are many different ways and reasons to engage with and to understand stakeholders. By far the most effective means of doing so is through direct two-way communication which can lead to a more in-depth understanding of how the organisation is viewed by stakeholders which ultimately will prevent a reputational crisis, and provide the organisation with tools to improve its operating procedures.

8.3 Media Surveillance

Only a few decades ago most large companies employed staff to review all the newspapers and to cut out the stories about the company, its competitors, the industry, and a variety of other things such as legislation changes that might affect the company and supply these clippings to senior executives to brief them on changes and keep them informed. With the advent of the internet, news media organisations publish nearly everything online, and now often news media organisations also include some stories developed on social media in their content. However that is not to say that social media will include all relevant information or all information that would be relevant to reputational crises.

Effective media surveillance to reduce the likelihood of a reputational crisis occurring should include collecting data on news media from sources including but not limited to:

- Social media,
- Google alerts,
- Newspapers,
- Television,
- Radio,
- Periodicals, and
- Newsletters.

It is good practice to source this data from a variety of news media organisations and types of media, because different news media organisations cater to different audiences. Thus some will choose to publish a story that other news media organisations will not. If all news media organisations are publishing a story on your organisation, then it is mostly likely dangerously close to a reputational crisis developing.

With the development of internet based news and social media, a number of media searching and collating software programs have become available. Many of these are subscription based and are readily available online. Some more advanced options in these programs will allow for a combination of specific search terms, collecting the information, and sorting the news media according to your preferences. These are also helpful tools in developing a concept in how stakeholders might view your organisation.

As all reputational crises are unique, it can be difficult to determine what the warning signs are in news media, if the stories don't relate specifically to your organisation. Some key elements are strong indicators that there should be cause for concern, namely;

- Protests,
- Embargos,
- Concerns regarding ethical practices of the organisation,
- Concerns regarding ethical practices of competitors,
- Concerns regarding ethical practices in relatable sectors,
- Other stakeholder activity,
- Increasing government oversight,
- Changes in legislation,
- Increasing fines for malpractice,
- Changes in best practice methods,
- Product concerns
- Service concerns
- Concerns regarding the organisation's longevity
- Changes in competitor behaviours and attitudes,
- Changes in downstream and upstream risks,

- Changes in stakeholder activities,
- Changes in stakeholder alliances,
- Changes in stakeholder viewpoints,
- Changes in stakeholder salience,
- Reputational crises in other industries that could relate to the organisation's industry,
- Reputational crises in the organisation's industry,
- Previous reputational crises (as these stories could spawn a new crisis),
- Changes in sentiment with consumers, politicians, suppliers, media, and other salient stakeholders, and
- Other relevant changes.

The list above seems extensive but is in actually a very basic and limited list of pre-crisis indicators. A complete list of indicators to scan for in the media would be organisation specific, making it impossible to develop a comprehensive yet generic list of indicators without filling up fifty pages.

In summary, any number of factors can be the impetus for a reputational crisis, and although it often takes more than one issue to create a reputational crisis, a single act or event can be suddenly considered offensive, and the reputational crisis can be unstoppable. The most effective media scanning will nearly always either stop a crisis from occurring, and at the very least minimize crisis impacts on the organisation and its stakeholders.

8.4 Ethical Data Management

In recent years data management issues have become a significant issue for large organisations. Through the development of online communities and enhanced data searching tools (including news media scanning software); organisations can find themselves in a reputational crisis through issues with:

- Data security
- Data sharing
- Data collection and usage
- Data retention

Data Security problems can easily develop into reputational crises because so much private and personal data now exists on citizens, consumers, and other stakeholders. Data security issues can place an organisation at risk of a crisis through sharing inappropriate personal data that could be perceived as offensive, extremely private, financially critical, amongst many other concerns. Any of those concerns could have very significant impacts on an organisation's stakeholders, and the organisation will be held to account for losses, and lose stakeholder trust.

Data Sharing is becoming more common as nearly all organisations collect data on their stakeholders, and many companies now purchase data from other companies for the purposes of target marketing, research, customer enhancement programs, and so forth. Although nearly all organisations obtain their stakeholder's consent to terms and conditions when engaging with the organisation, a legally binding stakeholder's consent is often not an effective claim in defending an organisation's reputation in a crisis. It is prudent to ensure that the stakeholders are aware that data sharing is practices and the ramifications of that data sharing.

Data Collection and Usage is now common practice for nearly all organisations. Similarly as with data sharing, consent is often obtained from the stakeholders through an acceptance of terms and conditions. However, despite that the organisation obtained legal consent, it does not indemnify the organisation from claims of offensive data collection practices. As a basic example; let's say that an application for a frequent shopper membership programme with a supermarket always obtains consent for the company to collect customer data. An employee at the supermarket's head office might think that they could create more revenue by sending cheeky emails to all frequent shoppers who have previously purchased contraceptives to suggest they buy in bulk. This could easily lead to many, if not all frequent shopper programme members to cancel their membership immediately, and likely lead to a small reputational crisis as the business offended customer's privacy, albeit within the legally binding consent contract.

Data Retention practices have become a concern amongst many stakeholders and consumer activist groups. Numerous governments are now pursuing legislation to limit the amount of time that an organisation can retain data. Despite these legislative developments, many companies still do not completely understand the ethics of data management, data rights, and data ownership. Although an organisation might retain a stakeholder's data and have no future plans for the use of that data, it is easy to conceive that another company might purchase the organisation and have different plans for the data. For example; a large chain of retail pharmacies retains customer data for ease of customer service, inventory management, and even budget forecasts. But if that company is purchased by a health or life insurance company, there could be a significant risk to the customer's financial security if pharmacy's data is shared with its new owner. Data retention practices can be very useful for increasing an organisation's efficiency, effectiveness, and the value of the organisation. However, as legislation has in most instances not yet been fully formed to manage these practices, the ethical implications can be significant.

In summary, unethical or ill-considered data management practices can easily lead to a crisis as the result of stakeholders being offended. To decrease the likelihood of a reputational crisis, it is important for an organisation to be aware of all its stakeholders and have a thorough understanding of their individuals concerns, motivations, and goals.

8.5 Reputational Crisis Insurance

Crisis insurance is now offered by some of the larger international insurance companies. Often this type of insurance policy is only available in a customised format, and does carry a corresponding payable premium. Generally crisis insurance policies will include cover paying for the organisation to acquire a multitude of services for the duration of a crisis. These services often include buying media (advertising) space, fees relating to acquiring the services of a crisis communication specialist, and require the investment of significant public liability insurance. Some insurance policies cover the costs of media space purchasing up to the value of $10,000,000. However as crises tend to vary significantly between different industries and different sectors in those industries, the amount of media space required to communicate effectively with crisis stakeholders differs significantly.

Most crisis insurance policies require the organisation to have developed a crisis prevention plan and a crisis management plan, as well as continuous reviews of both these plans, which are then submitted to the insurer for policy assessment. In other words, insurance companies will use the information of these plans to limit their risk and calculate the likelihood of a payout, with the aim of adjusting the customised policy premium to suit those risks and costs.

The costs involved with purchasing reputational crisis insurance do for many organisations seem to outweigh the perceived likelihood of a reputational crisis occurring, and consequently these policies are not very popular. Most organisations assume that because they have not had a crisis yet, that a crisis will not occur. Unfortunately it is precisely that type of thinking that suggests they should purchase crisis insurance, for if it is predictable a crisis will occur then the organisation will do everything to avoid having a crisis in the first place.

8.6 Summary

For smaller organisations the cost of purchasing reputational crisis insurance may well be outside their current operating budgets. However effectively preparing for a reputational crisis using the abovementioned strategies are an effective way of:

- Reducing the likelihood of a crisis occurring,
- Reduce the extent of crisis impacts, and
- Creates good corporate governance practices through engaging with stakeholders and issues as they arise.

Even if it is unlikely that a reputational crisis will occur, it is good practice to engage with these crisis prevention strategies to ensure longevity of the organisation, and mutually beneficial stakeholder relationships.

Chapter 9
Crisis Preparedness Quiz

This section is a multiple choice quiz, not designed to fail a participant, but to highlight the ethos of successfully managing a precarious reputational crisis. Following the quiz are detailed answers to each question.

1. Our most important stakeholders are
   (a) Our shareholders
   (b) Our suppliers
   (c) Our customers
   (d) Our policy makers
   (e) Our employees
   (f) Community groups
   (g) The environment
2. Our ethos is
   (a) Same as our company slogan
   (b) What we think what everyone thinks we are about
   (c) What everyone thinks we are about
   (d) Who we want to be
3. The first stage of any crisis is
   (a) When our actions are in the media
   (b) Our share price drops
   (c) Protestors are at our front gate
   (d) We appear to have acted contrary to our ethos
   (e) Some stakeholders feel we have done the wrong thing

T. Schermer, *Reputational Crises Unspun*, https://doi.org/10.1007/978-981-16-5130-4_9

4. The crisis is finally completely over when
   (a) The share price has stabilised
   (b) All compensations and fines have been paid
   (c) We have taken preventative actions against future crises
   (d) All salient stakeholders are satisfied with our efforts
5. Our crisis communication messages are effective when
   (a) The mainstream media is repeating them
   (b) Our stakeholders are in agreeance with our messages
   (c) All staff understand our position
   (d) The Board of Directors is satisfied
   (e) We are complying with laws and Corporate Social Responsibility standards
   (f) Our salient stakeholders are supportive of our efforts
6. Our ethos can be best understood from the point of view of our
   (a) Board of Directors
   (b) CEO
   (c) Employees
   (d) Stakeholders
   (e) Anyone
7. Organisational values are reflected in the
   (a) Mission statement
   (b) Company logo
   (c) The front line staff
   (d) The operational management activities
   (e) The organisational team building exercises
8. Interest groups are relevant to the organisation because
   (a) They are a threat to the organisation
   (b) They represent a significant proportion of the social environment in which we operate
   (c) They are stakeholders
   (d) The media repeats their claims
   (e) They are not relevant all the time
9. Every crisis is an opportunity to improve the organisation through
   (a) Making money out of solving the problem
   (b) Greater integration into the social environment in which we operate
   (c) Showing everyone who is in charge
   (d) Creating a new higher standard of best practice
   (e) Corporate restructure and corporate buy out

10. All crises can be managed better because
    (a) All crises are foreseeable
    (b) Crises are an opportunity to improve the way things are done
    (c) Until every stone has been turned, there must be better solutions
    (d) We can get reputational crisis insurance to offset negative effects from doing something wrong
    (e) We can improve the way the media interprets our messages
11. The rapid response news cycle and instant social media coverage means that
    (a) Crises can develop quickly
    (b) Crises can be resolved equally fast
    (c) Every crisis now develops quickly
    (d) We can identify salient stakeholders as they develop
    (e) We can respond instantly to any and all issues
12. A crisis cannot exist
    (a) Without media or social media coverage
    (b) Without stakeholders
    (c) Without salient stakeholders
    (d) Without actually doing something wrong
13. Any crisis can
    (a) End our organisation
    (b) Create an opportunity to create more revenues or profits
    (c) Give our organisation free media coverage
    (d) Give our organisation the opportunity to showcase it is better than others
14. Crisis panels are a great way to
    (a) Hand organisational control to interest groups
    (b) Develop a cohesive and comprehensive crisis outcome plan
    (c) A great way to lose shareholder confidence
    (d) Great to disempower and alienate organisational executives
    (e) Test key messages and themes to protect our bottom lines
15. It is good strategy to alienate stakeholders if they choose to
    (a) Point out the organisation's failures in the media
    (b) Selectively force our hand into cooperation
    (c) Make themselves unimportant
    (d) Work against us
    (e) Organise interest group amalgamation
    (f) Make themselves more important than our organisation

16. In theory, every crisis can be foreseeable because
    (a) We can look at the entire industry and learn from others
    (b) We can understand our own mission and where we are going
    (c) We are too big to fail
    (d) There is nothing new under the sun
    (e) No. not every crisis is foreseeable nor something for which we can strategize. We can only do our best

9.1 Answers to Crisis Preparedness Test

1. Our most important stakeholders are ALL. It doesn't help to use one answer for any number of situations. In some crises, the shareholders might be most important. Though often the most important stakeholder can be anyone. For instance, you might even have an employee who holds shares and chairs an interest group. It is best to look at each situation with a fresh perspective.
2. Our ethos should be (a) reflected in the company slogan, not the other way around. Our ethos should also be what we believe what everyone thinks we are about, so (b) is also true. Though it is risky to assume that you know what everyone thinks. It is better to engage with stakeholders and (c) ask them what they think we are about. It is helpful to have goals and ambitions (d), but goals and ambitions are about the future, and the current ethos is not there yet. So that would be a false claim. Consider framing it differently, but include those aspirations in your ethos.
3. The first stage of any crisis is often not (a) when the actions are in the media. By then, stakeholders, government agencies and interest groups are likely already engaged with the issue. The share price (b) often drops when the crisis has already started, and the media is engaging with the issue. Most crises have already started when (c) protestors are at the front gate, because it mostly takes a number of people to take offense to the organisation's actions, and those have taken offense who then have to find each other, and then organise themselves to protest at a time in the future.

   When you have acted contrary to your ethos, you might have a problem. When you "appear" to have acted contrary to your ethos, someone has observed it and has already developed the idea that you appear to have acted badly. This could lead to a reputational crisis. Similarly, when (e) some stakeholders feel you have done the wrong thing, it could lead to a crisis, if the stakeholders concerns aren't taken seriously, and dealt with in a respectful manner.
4. The crisis may be finally completely over when the (a) share price has stabilised as this often signals the end of the stage of (b) agreeing to pay compensation and fines. And although often (c) preventative measures to avoid a similar crisis may appease some stakeholders, some (d) salient stakeholders may not feel that is enough, and utilise the recent media attention to gain political support to have

fines and/or compensation reviewed to increase, or demand a resolution to disputes regarding preventative measures. Salient stakeholders should be satisfied to ensure the crisis won't flare up again.

5. Our crisis communication messages are not necessarily effective when the (a) mainstream media is repeating them. It might just be that the media is trying to enflame the situation to develop the story further. When the message has the support of (b) all your stakeholders, you are well on your way to crisis resolution. It is great if (c) the staff understands your position, however it doesn't mean the staff supports the position, and if other stakeholders don't support it, the crisis will definitely continue. After all, the staff are stakeholders as well. Although the (d) Board of Directors may be satisfied, other stakeholders may not agree and pursue government policy changes, or even demand that the Board of Directors be stood down for improper conduct. A crisis can topple any and all positions in an organisation. When all (e) laws have been complied with it doesn't mean you are getting ahead in the crisis. Laws nearly always fall short of instructing on good standards. Similarly, corporate social responsibility standards should never be viewed as a catch all method to ensure that all salient stakeholders are happy. It is only when (f) all salient stakeholders are supportive of the efforts, that it is likely to be safe, that the messages are effective, and you can move forward.
6. Our ethos can be best understood from the point of view of (e) anyone. It means nothing to customers, suppliers, or lobbyists if the (a) Board of Directors is happy. Nor do those people care if the (b) CEO is pleased with the ethos. The(c) employees, though critical in terms of going forward, are not the only salient stakeholders in a crisis. And as discussed in the stakeholder section, not everyone is a (d) stakeholder at every stage of the crisis. Thus someone who is not a stakeholder at the chronic crisis stage may be a stakeholder later during the crisis resolution stage (e.g. asbestosis compensation claims often occurred after the crises). This could fuel the crisis to flare up again. It is best if the organisational ethos can be well understood from anyone's perspective. This removes the risk of alienating someone who could be a salient stakeholder during any stage.
7. Organisational values are reflected in the (a) mission statement, (b) company logo, (c) front line staff, (d) operational management activities, (e) organisational team building exercises. Everything. If your organisational values are reasonable, and they resonate in everything you do, it will be easy to end a reputational crisis, as any crisis will only be accidental, or a misjudgement following years of good judgement. This is a key strategy to avoiding a lengthy and costly reputational crisis.
8. Interest groups are relevant to the organisation because they can (a) be a threat to the organisation. They also (b) represent a significant proportion of the environment in which we operate, and they are (c) stakeholders. The (d) media may repeat their claims. They may not be relevant all the time, but they (e) are relevant some of the time. It is risky to denounce the relevance of an earlier stakeholder as they may find themselves in a salient position later.

9. Every crisis is an opportunity to improve the organisation through (a) making money out of solving the problem. Most often crises develop because of a problem that needs to be solved. In many cases, solving the problem and crisis will at least require strategies such as preventative measures. Such measures may include improving the workplace health and safety, improving data security, managing oil spills, improving customer service and quality control, and so forth. The media coverage from the crisis gives the organisation a media opportunity to show the world how to be better than the best. This could be a free promotional opportunity for introducing the new standards and preventative measures system that the organisation has developed. For example, following the Deep Water oil spill in the Gulf of Mexico, BP created a separate company specialising in oil spill containment and clean ups. Somewhat similarly, Dreamworld, the theme park in Australia could have taken the reigns in their crisis following the drowning of several people on one of their rides. Instead of just trying to be better, they could have (d) taken the reigns and developed a new higher standard for safety in theme parks, and consulted other theme parks on how to improve their customer safety.

   A crisis is an opportunity to have (b) greater integration into the social environment in which we operate, through increasing stakeholder communication and engagement. Albeit under straining circumstances, a crisis does create an opportunity to (c) take charge of the situation to improve things. For example it creates many opportunities for an organisation to communicate and work together with the social environment in which it operates.

   During a reputational crisis a company's share price can become extremely volatile and change significantly many times during just one day. Thus it does create opportunities for others to (e) purchase the company. However new owners and a change of company name and banner do not make the company safe from future crises. Should the company be held to account for a similar crisis after the acquisition and rebranding, the media will make the connection to the organisation's past and most likely report it as *them trying to get away with the same thing, under a different banner.*

   Often organisations restructure following a reputational crisis. Such changes regularly include replacing the CEO, some Board members, and the creation of new divisions. Though prima facie this seems like a good move, it does little to change the organisational culture and values which allow the crisis to develop. It is more likely that the employees will feel somewhat displaced as a result the restructure, and as a result, be less likely to deal with ambiguous situations, such as situations that arise during a crisis.
10. All crises can be managed better, but (a) not because they are foreseeable. It is naïve and impossible to foresee all crisis events. However, (b) crises do present opportunities to improve the way things are done. By the simple logic that crisis events most often result from failures. Be it failures in safety, from proper oversight, or even from ethical disciplines. Crisis events highlight weaknesses and allow for improvement through training, operating procedures, ethical standards, media engagement, stakeholder engagement, and so forth. Unfortunately

contemporary crisis management and communication strategies stop short of trying to be great. The simple philosophy of seeking to be the (c) best is too often disregarded in the attempt to end the crisis as quickly as possible, at any cost. Until every stone has been turned, there must be better solutions for dealing with most issues.

Reputational crisis insurance is designed to reduce the impact of costs involved with dealing with a crisis. This type of insurance generally covers the cost of crisis consultants and buying related media space, but does not cover the costs of losses resulting from business interruptions, compensations, or fines. Although often companies can reduce the share market impact of business interruptions, and other crisis expenses such as fines (MarketWatch, 2019).

As practice makes perfect, crisis events (e) improve the way we communicate with media, through both immense increase in practice and because the organisation's focus on the media during crisis events.

11. The rapid response news cycle and instant social media coverage means that (a) crises can (c) develop quickly. A rapid and sizeable increase in online activity can quickly escalate an issue from social media to traditional media and dominate news headlines.

    However, proper online engagement with social media can also aid to (b) resolve issues equally fast. Efficient and (d) appropriate responses can deal with stakeholder concerns effectively, and oftentimes (e) resolve issues before they turn into crises.
12. A crisis (a) can exist without media or social media coverage. Although it may seem that a situation is not a crisis if it is not in the mainstream media, a crisis exists if an organisation is held to account for an offensive act. For example, a large protest or boycott without media coverage is still a reputational crisis that can shut down an organisation. However, (b) without stakeholders that can affect the organisation, or can be affected by the organisation, there is no crisis. In this scenario, it is prudent to (c) ensure that there are no affected stakeholders that could become important in the future.

    Often the most unexpected crisis events are those where the (d) organisation has done nothing wrong. Yet doing nothing wrong does not guarantee that an organisation will not be held to account for something it may or may not have done. Nor (d) does always doing what seems to be the right thing preclude the organisation from being held to account for one of those things, and that being considered offensive, thus leading to a crisis.
13. Any crisis can have an impact. Not all crises (a) end organisations. Often organisations survive for some time after a crisis, albeit in a diminished capacity. Possibly the biggest mistake most organisations make during a crisis, is underestimate the possible impact. Great examples of this is BP's reaction in the first few weeks of the Deepwater Horizon oil spill, which later saw the company's share price drop by more than 50% (Sabet et al., 2012). Cambridge Analytica, as arguably the most powerful public relations company in the world, underestimated its crisis when it was held to account, and the company ultimately closed its doors (Solon, 2018).

A crisis can (b) create opportunities to create more revenues and profits through learning from the issues and create better operating models. These may be in the form of reducing accidents, reducing regulatory fines and impediments through being better corporate citizens, reducing environmental impacts, or even through developing best practice methods for its operations and consulting for industry on how to avoid those crisis causing problems.

As most crises get phenomenal (c) mainstream media coverage, although often in a negative light, corporations can use the media platform to show remorse, corrective action, and best practice.

Although a crisis mostly occurs as a result of wrong doing, it is an (d) opportunity to show how the organisation can be better than it was before, and better than the rest. However this strategy must be exercised with a lot of caution as stakeholders become extremely unforgiving if an organisation tries to profit with free media which came about as a result of suffering it caused.

14. Crisis panels are a great way to engage with interest groups as they are a platform for all stakeholders, including the organisation, to discuss issues in a setting of equality. This definitely does not (a) mean handing over organisational control to interest groups. Instead, it empowers stakeholders to contribute to a (b) cohesive and comprehensive crisis outcome plan, as opposed to a limited focus being forced on everyone affected. A comprehensive crisis outcome plan can manage expectations of all stakeholders thus (c) increasing shareholder confidence.

    The crisis panel platform demands equality, and consequently organisational executives may feel disempowered during the panel proceedings. However (d) executive control of the organisation is maintained by the executives and the actual application of crisis panel recommendations remains in control of the executives.

    Crisis panels can be useful to discover the effectiveness and reception of key media messages and themes, which in the long term protect the corporate bottom lines.

15. It is good strategy to alienate stakeholders if they choose to somehow stop being a stakeholder in any way ever again. In other words never (a) alienate a stakeholder. Even though they may at times seem to make themselves redundant, they could in an unforeseen way very quickly escalate to a powerful position. For example, quiet often interest group members decide to quit their membership, and instead run for public office, and sometimes become a minister for the exact sector for which they were lobbying.

    Instead seek to become more integrated so that when a stakeholder points out an organisation's failures, sincerely try to understand their viewpoint. Somewhere in their argument is likely to be logical concern for an issue within your organisation. When a stakeholder (b) selectively forces cooperation, there is no choice but to comply. It is better to embrace this situation and the opportunity to show good corporate citizenship through cooperation.

    Simply, never alienate a stakeholder, even if for no other reason than that the stakeholder may come into a position of great influence and power.

16. In theory, every crisis can be foreseeable because, well, no. If a crisis is foreseeable, we would plan to avoid it in the first instance. If a crisis event is likely, we take further step to avoid it, and to mitigate the negative impacts, and learn from what happened.

    (a) Industry scanning for previous and current crises provides a good starting point to become aware of industry risks, enabling crisis prevention planning. Particularly if we (b) understand our own mission very well and are focussed on it, it is often more difficult to take a different viewpoint, including those viewpoints that might illuminate crisis risks.

    Over the past decades numerous large companies failed, and even the most powerful companies can fail. Again Cambridge Analytica is a great example as it managed public perception on issues in entire countries, yet it was unable to manage its image when in crisis and it failed. Interviews with the Cambridge Analytica executives underscore how the single minded perspective is very problematic in a crisis as it nearly always antagonises stakeholders. Quite simply, for as long as we have a singular perspective (d) we will find nothing new under the sun, thus leading us to antagonise stakeholders in a crisis.

    Being able to understand things from every stakeholder's perspective would be a perfect scenario. Unfortunately we can't possibly do that within time constraints and our own biases and prejudices. Consequently we can only do our best through better stakeholder relationships, being open minded to understand the perspectives of others, and build good ethics and good will into our organisations. And last but not least, try to be the best, though not through forcing the staff to toe the line, but more through inspiring our staff to build and be part of an organisation that is determined to do good, and lead with the best practices, to make sure that everyone is a winner.

Bibliography

MarketWatch. (2019, July 24). *Facebook earnings include admission of two antitrust probes and billions in fines, but stock barely hurt.* Retrieved July 30, 2019, from MarketWatch: https://www.marketwatch.com/story/facebook-earnings-include-admission-of-two-antitrust-probes-and-billions-in-fines-but-stock-still-gains-2019-07-24

Sabet, S., Cam, M., & Heaney, R. (2012). Sharemarket reaction to the BP oil spill and the US government moratorium on exploration. *Australian Journal of Management, 37*(1), 61–76.

Solon, O. (2018, May 3). *Cambridge Analytica closing after Facebook data harvesting scandal.* Retrieved July 29, 2019, from The Guardian: https://www.theguardian.com/uk-news/2018/may/02/cambridge-analytica-closing-down-after-facebook-row-reports-say.

Index

A
Acceptable, 9
Activists, x
Administrative, 10
Advertising, 53, 61, 68, 72, 148
Afterthought, 10
Agenda
  corporate, 63
  political, 56, 70
Agreement, 29, 113
Airbags, 132
Airline, 8
Alcoholics anonymous, 100
Allegiance, 52, 53, 144
Amusement park, 8
Angry, 118
Animal liberation, 10
Anxious, 118
Apologising, 89
Assets, 35
Attorneys, 10
Attributed, 7
Attribution theory, 33

B
Bank of America, 35
Board, 26, 37
Board of directors, 58, 111, 131, 137
Boeing, 132
Boycott, 36, 155
Bread, 8
British Petroleum (BP), 14, 17, 19, 21, 28, 32, 51, 53, 63, 76, 83, 101, 132, 154
Building companies, 36
Bush, 71, 72
Byron Bay Cookies, 19, 24, 25, 130

C
Cadbury, 52, 130
Cambridge analytica, 82
Campaign, 4
Capital, 35
Capital investment, 36
CEO, 14, 15, 26, 58, 73, 75, 93, 94, 123, 127, 132, 133, 150, 153, 154
Chickens, 72
Citizens, 8
Collective, 15, 50, 56, 63, 64, 69, 109
Commitment, 53, 122
Communications managers, ix
Compensation, 36
Construct, 13
Consultant, ix, 58, 117, 127, 130, 131
Contract, 138, 147
Corporate social responsibility (CSR), v, vi, 49, 55, 56, 94, 104, 105, 108, 122, 131, 132, 153
Crisis call centre, 128, 129
Crisis insurance, 148
Culture, v, 64, 90

D
Data management, 146–147
Decision tree, 118
Decorum, 111

T. Schermer, *Reputational Crises Unspun*, https://doi.org/10.1007/978-981-16-5130-4

Directors
  company, ix
Disasters, 7
Dishonest, 24, 29
Dividends, 36
Dreamworld, 102, 154

E
Ego, 98, 117, 137
Email, 117, 147
Empathy, 14, 29, 50–51, 62, 89, 92, 119, 120, 122, 123, 129, 133
Encumbent politicians, 61
Environment, 9
Environmentalist, 35
Ethics, 49, 56, 70, 104, 147, 157
Ethos, 118, 131
Evidence, 20, 31, 72, 82
Explosion, 24, 121

F
Facebook, 4, 82
Fault, 26, 121
Fees, 148
Filtration equipment, 35
Fines, 35, 36, 102, 122, 132, 133, 145
Fourth Estate, 53
Framing, 68, 69, 71, 72, 117, 123, 130, 152
Frustrated, 118
Funds, 36

G
Germany, 72
Goebbels, 72
Governance, 50, 54, 56–58, 96, 104, 148
Gulf of Mexico, 34
Gutenberg, 71

H
Hate speech, 36
Hitler, 72
Hofstede, 90
  Geert, 90
Holistic, 14
Honest, 62, 144
Honesty, 6

I
IBM, 15, 90
Illegal, 46, 113
Image, 14
Incumbent politicians, 62
Injured, 58
Insurance, 17, 58, 142, 147
Integrity, vii, 62, 104
Interim profits, 35
International Organisation for Standardization, 104
Interrelationship, 33
Investment, 58, 63, 148
Iraq, 71
ISO 26000, 94, 104, 105

J
Jeremy Clarkson, 83, 99, 124
Journalists, 83, 117

K
Killed, 118, 132

L
Laws, 8
Lawyers, 60
Legal, 29, 58, 60, 63, 74, 92, 94, 97, 120, 121, 129, 147
Legally bound, 10
Legislative bodies, 10
Legislators, 61, 63, 82, 84, 103, 124, 133
Liability, 29, 92, 121, 148
Logging, 9
Losses, 60, 62, 94, 146, 155

M
Mainstream media, 7
Malaysian airlines, 132
Malfeasance, 32
Mark Zuckerberg, 4
Martin Luther King, 73
Media statement templates, 107
Mediated, 11
Member of parliament, 8
Metgasco, 19
Mining, 35
Moratorium, 19, 53, 63

N
News media information packet, 131
Newspapers, 37, 144
News values, 124

O
Offensiveness, 9
Out group, 74, 76
Outrage, 35
Outsource, 55, 96
Ownership, 36

P
Perceptions, 6
Phenomena, 13
Philosophical differences, 8
Photo, 72, 74, 130, 131
Pizza, 36
Polarisation, 18, 72
Political allies, 5
Political lobbyists, 58
Politicians, 8
Practical approach, 79
Profit, 18, 22, 47, 51, 83, 100
Profitability, 17, 35
Profitable, 36
Promiscuous, 8
Propaganda, 71, 72
Public perception, 11
Public prosecutors, 58
Public relations, vi, 72, 82, 86, 117, 120, 155
Punitive, 34

R
Racial, 73
Readership, 11
Recall, 123, 128, 129
Recurring, 23, 24, 32, 62
Regret, 27, 29
Regulator, 34
Restructure, 8
Revenue, 35
Right words, 6
Rokeach, M., 90
Rules, 91, 104–105, 111, 123, 127

S
Safety, 14, 19, 32, 59, 102, 103, 112, 123, 128, 131
Salience, 24, 46–48, 56–62, 96, 142–144, 146
Scandals, 7
Scanning, 17, 19–23, 146, 157
Shareholder's interests, 36
Shareholders, 9, 58
Share price, 34–37, 83, 94, 122, 132, 149, 150, 152, 154, 155
Social contract, 138
Social media strategies, 6
Social welfare groups, 10–11
Society, 27, 49, 55, 57, 60, 68, 70, 73–75, 85, 90, 91, 97, 98, 104, 105, 122, 133, 138
Solving reputational crises, 107
Spatial gap, 71
Stability, 24, 28, 31, 32, 119, 127
Stakeholder group, 112, 121
Stakeholder legitimacy, 60
Stakeholder power, 60
Stakeholder representatives, 110, 113, 117
Stakeholders, 45
Stakeholder urgency, 60
Strawberries, 8
Surveillance, 145
Symbiotic, 105

T
Telephone, 96
Terrorism, 72
Terrorist, 18, 72
Tertiary stakeholders, 10
Time critical, 7
Toyota, 132
Trade union, 10
Transcendence, 27, 30
Triple bottom line, vi, 104, 108

U
Upset, 40, 51, 92, 119, 120

V
Values, 15, 29, 46, 51, 73, 74, 90, 91, 104, 131
Virgin airlines, 15
Volkswagen, 24, 35, 38, 132, 133

W
War, 16, 72
Wealth, 10
WHIG, 72
White House, 56, 70, 72
Wrongful action, 6